HALF PRICE BOOKS®

Half Price Books
1835 Forms Drive
Carrollton, TX 75006
OFS OrderID 39900437

Thank you for your order, ABE APTP Order!

Thank you for shopping with Half Price Books! Please contact service87@hpb.com. if you have any questions, comments or concerns about your order (741755523)

Visit our stores to sell your books, music, movies games for cash.

SKU	ISBN/UPC	Title & Author/Artist	Shelf ID	Qty	OrderSKU
S463829405	9780871952592	The Scenic Route: Stories from the Heartland Foreword by Frank and Katrina Basile	REG3.1	1	

SHIPPED STANDARD TO:
ABE APTP Order
800 Avondale Ave
6EW35GFG
Columbus OH 43212
help@textbookrush.com

ORDER# **741755523**
Abebooks

AF825559

The Scenic Route
Stories from the Heartland

The Scenic Route
Stories from the Heartland

Foreword by
Frank and Katrina Basile

INDIANA HISTORICAL SOCIETY PRESS
INDIANAPOLIS 2007

Printed in Canada

This book is a publication of the
Indiana Historical Society Press
450 West Ohio Street
Indianapolis, Indiana 46202-3269 USA
www.indianahistory.org

Telephone orders 1-800-447-1830
Fax orders 317-234-0562
Online orders @ shop.indianahistory.org

The paper in this publication meets the minimum
requirements of American National Standard for
Information Sciences—Permanence of Paper for
Printed Library Materials, ANSI Z39.48-1984.

Library of Congress Cataloging-in-Publication Data

The scenic route : stories from the heartland/ edited by Ellen
Munds and Beth Millett.

p. cm.
ISBN 978-0-87195-259-2 (pbk. : alk. paper) 1. Middle
West—Social life and customs—20th century—Anecdotes.
2. Middle West—Biography—Anecdotes. 3. Indiana—Social
life and customs—20th century—Anecdotes. 4. Indiana—
Biography—Anecdotes. 5. Children—Middle West—Social life
and customs—20th century—Anecdotes. 6. Storytellers—
Middle West—Biography—Anecdotes. I. Munds, Ellen. II.
Millett, Beth.
F355.S29 2007
977'.0330922—dc22 2007012374

The Scenic Route: Stories from the Heartland is made possible
by a generous grant from Frank and Katrina Basile

Foreword

When Bob Sander, cofounder of Storytelling Arts of Indiana, invited me to join its board in 1996, I accepted with enthusiasm since I had been telling stories as a professional speaker since 1971. I then met the other two cofounders, Ellen Munds and Nancy Barton, who with Bob had started the organization in Indianapolis in November 1987.

I was privileged to serve on the board for five years, two as president, and have continued to attend events and to keep up-to-date with what is happening with the organization. It has been a joy to witness its progress during the last ten years. During that time I was fortunate to have had the opportunity to sponsor both the 1999 Storyteller's Theatre and Storytelling Festival. In 1999 Ellen developed the idea for an Emerging Stories Fellowship to encourage and recognize Indiana storytellers. She presented me with the opportunity to sponsor this program, which I have had the pleasure of doing since its inception in 2000.

Celebrating its twentieth anniversary under the capable direction of its Executive Director, Ellen Munds, Storytelling Arts has been actively promoting the art and use of storytelling in daily life through its annual festival, concerts, workshops, programs, and other events.

I am pleased that Ellen gave my wife, Katrina, and me the opportunity to sponsor this book to commemorate the twentieth anniversary. It contains wonderful stories by twelve outstanding storytellers, four of whom are past recipients of the Emerging Stories Fellowship.

The performance home of the organization is the Indiana History Center, whose motto is "Indiana's Storyteller—Connecting People to the Past." There is no better way to communicate a state's history, a family's history, or a company's history than through storytelling. In the twenty years that I wrote a weekly column for the *Indianapolis Business Journal*, I wrote many articles about storytelling and its use and importance in business and everyday life.

Storytelling Arts has helped the citizens of Indiana during the past twenty years by providing opportunities to enjoy storytelling while also learning to be better storytellers.

Frank and Katrina Basile

Contents

ix **FOREWORD**
Frank and Katrina Basile

xi **PREFACE**
Ellen Munds and Beth Millett

1 **JUMP ROPE KINGDOM**
Mary Hamilton

5 **RUDY AND THE ROLLER SKATE**
Dan Keding

13 **THE POSSUM SKIN HAT**
Bob Sander

25 **BICYCLE RACE**
Bill Harley

35 **SOME ENCHANTED WEDNESDAY**
Syd Lieberman

43 **THE MAN WHO PLANTED TREES**
Liza Hyatt

53 **OLD AUBBEENAUBBEE AND THE MULTIFUNCTION BOY SCOUT KNIFE**
George Schricker

67 **GRANDPA'S BARN**
Jim May

83 **THE PIPELINE BLUES: A MIDWEST STORY OF ENVIRONMENTAL TRIUMPH**
Beth Horner

97 **SOME CALLED HIM DOC**
Lou Ann Homan

101 **THE LAST FIVE MINUTES**
Nancy Donoval

109 **THE RAINMAKER**
Michael Cotter

Preface

Storytelling is about gathering with friends, family, and even those we've just met to share with one another stories of our childhood, our culture, and our heritage. In this day and age of overscheduled lives, Internet and television addictions, and outside pressures, sharing and listening to stories reminds us of our humanity. Whether it's stories about childhood pranks or the ethnic rituals of holiday celebrations, the art of storytelling slows us down and keeps those memories and traditions alive.

Storytelling Arts of Indiana has spent twenty years creating places for individuals to come together and experience storytelling in the hope of encouraging that sharing and listening relationship in our everyday lives. To celebrate our twentieth anniversary, we've collected stories from a dozen storytellers who have graced our stages and who share our midwestern heritage. We hope you enjoy them as much as we do!

Ellen Munds, executive director
Beth Millett, president

JUMP ROPE KINGDOM
Mary Hamilton

First grade babies
Second grade tots
Third grade angels
Fourth grade snots
Fifth grade peaches
Sixth grade plums
And all the rest are dirty bums

I heard that rhyme for the first time on my first day of school—the first day of first grade at Flaherty Elementary in Meade County, Kentucky. I'm not sure who started it. Could have been the snots. They were proud of themselves. Might have been the peaches. Might have been the plums. I don't believe it was the dirty bums because, if memory serves me correctly, the dirty bums were considered much too old for recess.

I heard the rhyme day after day, recess after recess. Even when the bell rang and our teachers left the school building to meet us and we ran from the playground to meet our teachers, the rhyme did not stop. As the other first graders and I followed our teacher in single file to our classroom, I could still hear that rhyme, now a whispered taunt:

First grade babies
Second grade tots
Third gr—

I was in first grade, but I was not a baby. I was the only child in my family old enough to walk all the way out our long winding gravel driveway, catch the big yellow school bus, and ride it to school. I wasn't a baby. I was a big girl. But somehow I knew if I said "Teacher, teacher, do you hear. . ." there would be laughter, and I wouldn't think it was funny. The big kids were the ones who chanted the rhyme, and at my school the big kids ruled the playground.

The big boys ruled the kingdom of marbles—marbles, a game played in rings drawn in dust beneath the shade of trees. I can't tell you what happened in the kingdom of marbles; when I was a girl, marbles was a boys-only world.

The big girls ruled a kingdom too. They ruled the jump rope kingdom—they decided who was going to turn the rope, who was going to jump, what chants were going to be chanted.

When I began first grade, I knew how to jump rope—I did! Mama would tie a rope to a porch post, and then she would string the rope across the porch. My little sister Patty would pick up the other end of the rope. I'd stand beside the rope and watch Patty. She would turn the rope and I would jump. I knew how to jump rope when I began first grade.

But in the jump rope kingdom ruled by the big girls, no one stood beside the rope and waited for the rope to turn. Oh no, the big girls ran in while the rope was turning. They ran in chanting the words of the jump rope rhymes:

Not last night but the night before
Twenty-four robbers came a-knocking at my door.
As I ran out, (the big girl ran out)
They ran in (she jumped back in, called "going in the back door")
And hit me on the head with a rolling pin
And this is what they said for me to do
Fancy Dancer, do the twist (the big girl twisted while she jumped)
Fancy Dancer, give a high kick (she'd kick and jump on one foot)
Fancy Dancer, turn all around (she turned in a circle while she jumped)
Fancy Dancer, get out of town (the big girl would run out; the next would run in and the chant would begin again.)

The rope never stopped.

I was not prepared.

So I sat on the sidewalk and I watched. I learned the rhymes; I took them home; I taught them to my sister, but I did not jump rope with the big girls.

One day, one of the big girls, Anna Jo Hinton, walked over, looked down at me, and said,

"Don't you want to jump rope?"

"Oh, I do. I do, but"

"But you don't know how, do you?"

"Oh, I know how to jump. I know the rhymes and everything. I just don't know how to run in."

Anna Jo looked back at the other big girls, "Hey, she does too know how to jump. She just doesn't know how to run in. I believe I can teach her."

Some of the big girls laughed, but Anna Jo looked at me and offered her hand. "You hold my hand," she said, "and when I say run, you run. When I say jump, you jump."

I held her hand. "Run!" she said. I ran.

"Jump!" I jumped.

Missed—I missed. Some of the big girls laughed—at me—but Anna Jo silenced them with, "Hey, she almost got it. Turn the rope again."

And again—"Run!" I ran. "Jump!" I jumped. I wish I could tell you I succeeded on my second try, but it wasn't an easy thing for me to learn.

Over and over again, Anna Jo made the other big girls turn the rope, until. . .

"Run!" I ran.

"Jump!" I jumped,

and I was jumping rope!

Anna Jo looked at me and said, "You'd better hold my hand again. I'm going to have to teach you how to get out of here." And I stopped the rope several more times learning how to run out.

Anna Jo Hinton was a queen in the jump rope kingdom. A queen who could lead the other big girls with wisdom enough—and courage enough—to offer her hand to one they taunted as a first-grade baby and bring that first-grade baby all the way inside the Jump Rope Kingdom.

Mary Hamilton

Mary Hamilton, a Frankfort, Kentucky-based storyteller and workshop leader, grew up on a Kentucky farm where telling stories was considered a moral failing. After years of confessing her storytelling sins, she finally gave in to temptation and found her career. Since 1983 Hamilton has strengthened imaginations with her straightforward, just-talking storytelling style. When she takes the stage, worlds unfold in the hearts and minds of the audience. Learn more about her work, including how you can order her recording of "Jump Rope Kingdom" on her CD Some Dog and Other Kentucky Wonders, *at her Web site: www.maryhamilton.info/.*

RUDY AND THE ROLLER SKATE

Dan Keding

When I was a boy, I wanted a dog more than anything. All my friends could teach tricks to their younger brothers or sisters, but I was an only child. I thought a dog would fill in the gap nicely. Noni, my grandmother, was not so sure. She said that after a week or so, I would forget the dog and she would become the primary caregiver to yet another "child." No matter how I begged and pleaded, her answer was a resolute "No." Finally, one Christmas morning, after I had made a nuisance of myself the entire fall, it happened. There, under the tree, was a big box with holes punched in its sides and my name on the ribbon. Holding my breath, I waited until it was my turn to open a package. I dove for the box, ripped off the paper, and pried the top off. There it was—a turtle. My wonderful, though slightly addled, family had bought a wild and hyperactive third grader a turtle. As I lifted it out of the box it drew its legs and head into its shell. Great, now I was the proud owner of a big green "rock."

Noni looked at me hopefully. "Do you like it?"

Well, what can you say to someone who loves you? "Yes grandma, it's great."

I put the beast on the carpet and watched to see what it would do. Soon it emerged and started to explore its new world. I had an idea. I ran up to my room and grabbed a little red ball, the kind that was usually at the end of a long rubber band and attached to a paddle. Sitting down in front of the turtle, I began to bounce the ball right in front of his beady little eyes. As soon as I was sure I had his attention, I rolled the ball toward his stubby little beak. Snap! He took hold of it. I was ecstatic. I had a turtle that could fetch! Eager to see him do it again, I reached for the ball. I pulled, and I pried, and I even swung him around, but he just held on to that ball for all he was worth. What could I do? Well, it was obvious that fetching wasn't going to be his game, so I did the only thing a boy my age could do: I glued a plastic machine gun to the back of his shell and turned him into an armored personnel carrier.

Now I had the only living tank in Chicago. I played with my turtle for weeks. I'd line up my toy soldiers and he'd march right through them. Life with my new pet went pretty well until one sunny day in early spring. I was outside with my friends, surrounded by dozens of toy soldiers, and Noni called us all to lunch. By the time we got back to the yard, all of our carefully placed troops were all knocked down and the turtle was gone! We searched and searched, but he was missing in action.

Weeks passed, and then, one hot summer day, the turtle appeared in my Aunt

Mary's flower garden. He had gone wild. His red eyes were flashing and he still had that machine gun on his back. He opened his beak, stuck out his tongue, and hissed. We stepped back. You know, there is nothing more dangerous than a wild, armed turtle. We had to leave him in the garden. Who knows, maybe he's still there.

Noni and I were always together that summer. Wherever she went, I went—to the store, to church every morning, and to "parties." Noni loved "parties." Every morning, without fail, she read the obituaries in the *Daily News*. If anyone of Croatian descent had died we went to the wake. We hurried into our Sunday clothes, caught the next bus, and away we went to the "party."

Now, Noni wasn't satisfied with simply attending the wake. No, she had to make sure that someone there was in deep mourning. The minute she walked through the door she began to cry and talk to God in Croatian about what a tragedy this death was for all. The only problem with this was that nine out of ten times, Noni hadn't known the dead person at all. She would walk to the coffin holding my hand tightly and throw herself, and me in the process, over the body. Folks would help her to a seat and some kind soul would fan her. Later, watching their eyes, I was sure I could see it—the question, "Who is she?" But by the time this happened, we had signed the book and were stepping out the door.

I asked my Mom one day what she thought I could do about Noni's "problem." Mom just smiled and said, "If you can't beat 'em, join 'em."

I had no clue what she meant, but by the time of the next wake I was pretty sure I'd figured it out. When Noni collapsed over the coffin, I started to cry and moan, "Oh, what a great man. We're all going to miss him so much." Soon adults were swarming around me, patting me on the head and back, and telling me not to cry. One old man reached into his pocket and pulled out a dime. "Here. It will be all right," he said. "Buy yourself a candy bar."

Wake after wake, kind men with tears in their eyes gave me nickels and pennies. Ladies dressed in black and smelling of lilac and deodorant opened their pocketbooks and lovingly pressed coins into my hands. "Don't cry, dear. Get yourself a soda." I made sixteen dollars going to wakes that summer.

If we weren't going to wakes, baking bread, or doing the laundry, Noni and I were off for a visit with Teta Marica. She was a matriarch among my grandmother's set of friends, and now that Marica was older, we made a pilgrimage to her house every week. Noni and I boarded a bus and traveled into a neighborhood of bungalows, each identical to the next in almost every way. People joked that a drunk coming home could never find his own house unless he started at one end of the block and tried each door lock until the key finally fit.

Each time we visited Marica's, I ran up the steps to ring the bell. Soon she came to the door, always dressed in a long black skirt, a long-sleeved white blouse, and a shawl that she pulled up over her head whenever she went outside. She dressed this way in summer and in winter, her shawl a constant companion no matter how warm the weather.

"Dobra dan, Teta Marica. Kako si ve?"
"Ja sam dobra. Kako si ti, Daniel?"
"Dobra."

She always greeted me in Croatian. "Good day, how are you?" and "I am well." Then she opened the door wide and invited Noni and me to enter. Once inside, you always knew right where you were going. In fact, you probably couldn't get lost, even if you tried. There was a plastic runner that started at the front door, ran through the living and dining rooms, and ended at the kitchen door. On either side of it the furniture was covered in clear plastic, which Marica wiped down with Pine Sol at least twice a day. The place was so clean that a doctor could have done open-heart surgery on the couch. Every time I walked through to the kitchen, I wondered what might happen if I stepped off the runner. Would an alarm go off? I was tempted to try it, but decided to wait.

One day, when we got to the kitchen, Marica announced that she had a treat for us. She had just made donuts and had a fresh pot of coffee. Quickly, I glanced out of the corner of my eye at Noni's face. My grandmother was not keen on me having caffeine in my blood system. Now, I'm not saying I was a bad kid, but when I was in fifth grade, Sister Marie traded me to Sister Samuel for five students and a player-to-be-named-later. Sister Samuel swore to her dying day that she had been cheated. At home I drank Kool-Aid, not Coke or Pepsi, and coffee was completely off the "I-might-consider-that" list. But I was taught at a young age that when you are a guest in someone's home, you are polite and do as you are told. I took the coffee. Without hesitation, I poured in Carnation milk, straight from the can, and added four heaping spoonfuls of sugar. My coffee now was the consistency of Karo syrup. I took my first sip and I was hooked. Then Marica gave me a donut. She was famous for her donuts. As I raised it to my lips I heard her say, "Dunk it."

Now, I was taught to obey my elders, but when I heard those words I began to feel sick. I hated to mix foods. I didn't even want them to touch each other on my plate. I used some of my mashed potatoes to build walls between my meat and peas and ate only the "unspoiled" potatoes. To take one food and deliberately put it into another was unthinkable.

"I'm sorry Teta Marica, but I can't do that."

"It's good for you, go ahead."

Looking across the table, I could see a gleam of rightful revenge in Noni's face. Obviously this was the price I had to pay for drinking coffee. Beside, I was the only person at the table who still had real teeth. I wasn't going to win this one. I dipped the donut into my coffee and watched it become a mass of soggy dough. At this very moment, I heard a strange sound, something like a cow choking on a wad of its cud. I looked all around but saw nothing until I spied something under the table in the corner. There it was, a remarkable creature, long and brown with a grey face. But where were the legs? It sat, or lay—I couldn't really tell which—on a mound of carpets and blankets. In front of it there was a bowl filled with coffee and milk, a donut floating in the middle. I stared, but it was too busy trying to corral the floating donut to pay me any mind at all.

"What is that?"

"That's Rudy, my dog," Marica answered proudly.

"That's a dog?" I asked incredulously.

Marica didn't answer.

Still staring, I could see that Rudy was a standard dachshund. He did have legs—short, short, stubby legs—and he weighed about eighty pounds. There were scars and scabs all over his belly, and when he stood, the clearance between his stomach and the floor could only be measured in hundredths-of-an-inch. This dog gave new meaning to the word "huge."

I slowly finished my donut and coffee. After watching Rudy eat, they didn't taste so bad. Soon more ladies arrived and sat politely around the table. Like most immigrant kitchens, Marica's was almost as big as the living room. In some homes, people even knocked out a wall to another room so the kitchen could accommodate all of the people who gathered there for meals.

After coffee was served and the "hellos" and "how-are-yous" were said, all of the ladies turned to Noni and glanced at me. I knew it was time for me to go. They were ready for gossip but couldn't talk with me in the room. I was bilingual and they were afraid I might blackmail them. I had done it the year before. Noni stood up, took a leash off the back door knob, and handed it to me.

"Take the dog for a walk."
"The dog?" I hesitated. "Does it move?"

I thought this was a reasonable question. Noni didn't. She gave me that "do-it-now" look, and I snapped the leash on the dog and stepped out the back door.

Standing on the back porch, I faced our first obstacle, the stairs—all five of them. With every step I heard a sickening thud as Rudy's belly smacked the wooden step. Next, we walked through the gangway, that small sidewalk that runs between buildings. I hoped that the plague had taken out the neighborhood. I didn't want anyone to see me with this creature.

As we began our walk, Rudy moved at a snail's pace. The turtle was faster than this dog. No, I take that back, a tree was faster than this dog. He would waddle for three or four feet and then stop to catch his breath, inhaling and exhaling loud enough to be heard on the next block. During these bouts of breathing, his breath would come into contact with the outside air, and what a breath he had! He could kill a cockroach at four feet with a single puff. Then he would go over and eat it. Rudy ate anything that didn't move. I was careful never to take a nap when he was in the room. It took us about an hour to go around the block. By the time we got back, Noni was ready to go home.

Noni and I visited Marica every week, and every week I had to walk that dog. I hated it. The kids in Rudy's neighborhood were merciless in their teasing. They would shout, "You having fun?" or "Does that thing have legs?" I ignored them. It wasn't my neighborhood, but I knew the rules that most neighborhood kids follow. In no time, all talk about getting a dog of my own was over and Noni was one happy grandma.

One day, as Rudy and I were going on our slow walk down the street, I looked down, watching him move his sad little legs. "What you need, dog, is a set of wheels." I was thinking out loud, and in the next moment I was filled with inspiration. I had one metal roller skate, the kind that you clamped onto your shoe and tightened with a key, and an old beaded Indian belt from the Wisconsin Dells, made by a tribe in Korea. They would do nicely!

The next time Noni and I set off for Rudy's house, I crammed my skate, belt, and an old dish towel in a paper bag.

"What's in the bag?" Noni asked.

"Toys for Rudy."

"Good boy," she said, smiling.

I thought, "You don't know how good."

When it was time for the walk, I made sure that nobody in the house was watching. Once we were out in the yard, I looked down at Rudy, opened the bag, and said, "I have a gift for you, old boy." I put the skate down, rolled the towel up and placed it on top of the skate, lifted Rudy in the middle, and slid the skate underneath his ponderous paunch. Next, I wrapped the belt around the dog and the skate, tightened it, and we were off. I couldn't believe the difference. We weren't exactly running, but he was walking at a good pace. He looked up at me as if to say, "This is good."

Everything was going according to plan when we hit the hill that ran down to Archer Avenue. I had forgotten about this hill. We flew down, Rudy's ears flapping in the wind, and me trying to keep a hold on the leash that was attached to the runaway dog. Near the bottom, we wrapped ourselves around a telephone pole, and Rudy gave me a look that said, "Let's do it again!"

Rudy got to be really good at taking that hill. He tucked his front paws up under himself and kind of body surfed all the way down. Folks who used to ignore us were in awe of us now. Buses on Archer Avenue stopped, and the bus driver announced, "If you look out your windows, folks, you'll see a boy walking his dog on a roller skate." Everybody waved, and I waved back. Rudy, a little too proud to wave, just looked around with a smile. The policeman on the beat stopped and rubbed Rudy's ears, telling him what a good dog he was. The kids who used to tease me all the time started asking if they could walk the dog. I charged them a dime for one trip down the hill and used the money to buy dog biscuits. They never really helped his breath, but they sure made him happy.

Sometimes my new friends and I took Rudy across Archer to the park. A couple of us would carry him to the top of the slide while a few more waited at the bottom. That dog would speed down the slide and then, for the split second just before we caught him, he'd be airborne. Afterwards, we'd all sit in the shade of the huge elm trees and pet Rudy. We'd take off the roller skate and scratch his belly and his ears. He'd lie there and look at us as if to say, "I've waited my whole life for this summer." With half a dozen hands petting him, he'd drop off to sleep.

One day, just before school started in the fall, Rudy and I were racing down the hill when we came to a stop at the light on Archer. When the light changed to green, I tugged on the leash and said, "Come on, boy, let's go." But Rudy didn't move. I knelt down next to him; I knew that even with his roller skate on, you could barely tell if he was standing, sitting, or lying down.

"What's wrong, boy?" Rudy's eyes were closed and his body was still. He had taken his last walk. With tears falling down my face, I picked him up and carried him back up the hill to Marica's house. I took off the roller skate because no one in the house knew about it and rang the doorbell. Marica came out. I told her he was gone. She looked at him lying there in the sunlight, so peaceful on the grass, and the tears came down her beautiful cheeks.

"He was a good boy, wasn't he, Daniel?"

I didn't have to lie. "Teta Marica, he was the best, the very best."

And that is the true story of Rudy and the roller skate.

Dan Keding

Dan Keding grew up with folktales taught to him by his Croatian grandmother. His recordings have won numerous awards, such as the American Library Association's Notable Recording for Children. His book, Stories of Hope and Spirit, *won the prestigious Anne Izard Storyteller's Choice Award. A featured columnist for twenty years for* Sing Out Magazine, *his second book,* English Folktales, *was released in the fall of 2005. In 2000 Keding was honored with induction into The National Storytelling Network's Circle of Excellence. A sought-after performer, he continues to work at festivals, libraries, museums, schools, and universities around the world. For more information visit www.dankeding.com or contact him at dantale@earthlink.com.*

THE POSSUM SKIN HAT

Bob Sander

Walt Disney had it in for raccoons. He must have, because in late-1950s America, every boy wanted one—dead. More precisely: skinned and made into a cap. I was no exception. The banded tail of a Disney coon carcass made Fess Parker's Davy Crockett seem like a god. I was sure Davy-style fame could be mine, too, if I got one of those caps. I was hungry for Crockett-like glory, if not at the Alamo then at least in Beech Grove, the small central Indiana town where I grew up.

Thinking back on it, Disney productions were instrumental in several character-building moments of my youth. His movie version of *Old Yeller* emboldened me to entice a cur dog from her exertions in raiding a garbage can long enough for me to steal her meal (a discarded ham-hock) and lure her home.

"Can we keep her Mom? She looks just like Old Yeller!"
"We'll see. Where'd she come from?"
"An alley, I guess. She followed me home." (Technically, this was true.)

We had Yeller more than ten years. A day never went by that her mere presence reminded me of what value there is in being truthful and the usefulness of technicalities.

Then there was the Swiss Family Robinson. The way they fashioned found articles and items from nature into needed daily contrivances was a real marvel. Their successes led me to disassemble several household appliances and reform them into combinations hitherto unsuspected—especially by my awestruck parents.

Experiences of this sort stood me in good stead when I faced the challenge of how to procure a coonskin cap. The easiest way was simply to buy one. Nor was that beneath my dignity. I urged my parents to do just that. Urged them strenuously. But it was not to be. It all just played out wrong.

What happened was this: Our town's little one-screen theater was sandwiched between Herb's Men's Shop and the Standard Grocery. I went to see the Crockett movie there with my parents. I was on fire for one of those hats. Meanwhile Herb, of the adjacent Men's Shop, had pushed a cart out onto the sidewalk in front of his shop. It was stacked full of Crockett caps. Every boy who emerged from the theater was instantly driven insensible by the mere sight of those hats. So was I. But before I could decide on the correct brand of whining to bend my parents into compliance, my father one-upped me.

"Look at all those suckers!"

I looked at the scene again. It sounded too good to be true. Evidently there were not only Crockett caps to be had, but suckers too! I loved suckers, especially grape flavored ones.

"Look at 'em all, going for those caps like sheep being sheared in a pen. Herb's a sly one. It's like shooting fish in a barrel. Well—there's no suckers in this family. Right?"

"Not right now, Dad. But we could get one, maybe."

"No, no! We're not gonna fork over our money for one of those caps, are we?"

"N—Wait! We're not? How come?"

"'Cause. We're not suckers. He's got the price of those caps jacked up to the moon—and we know it."

"He does?"

"Sure he does. Only suckers would pay that much."

My passion for suckers had suddenly become complicated. Why (or how?) would a sucker pay for a coonskin cap? And there was something about the way he said the word: "suckers." Maybe not all suckers were the desirable treats I'd thought them to be. Whole different orders of suckers must exist, different than I imagined.

"Yeah, Dad. Only suckers."

"And we don't want to be one of them, do we?"

"Naw. Course not."

"That's right. Why, I bet we could come back here on Monday morning and pick those up for half price."

"The suckers?!"

"No—the hats!"

"No kidding?"

"Sure. He'll be begging to unload 'em then. Hey, what say we walk over to the drugstore? I want some shoe polish. And you can get a sucker if you want."

Life was pretty strange most of the time, but adding in words made it completely indecipherable.

Unfortunately, no caps were available the following Monday. Herb was completely sold out. My Dad blamed it all on "the suckers." I resolved to quit eating them for a while until I figured out how they had snookered me out of my cap.

Only my friend Steve and I were without Crockett hats. Every other kid in town seemed to have one. Some even had "Old Betsy" look-alike air rifles. We were mortified.

Steve posed the fateful question: "What would Davy do?"

Well, we quickly figured out what he wouldn't do: He sure as heck wouldn't go hanging around Herb's Men's Shop, hoping for a restock. Not Davy Crockett. Matter of fact, it occurred to us that the mere idea of Crockett buying from such an establishment was the height of lunacy. Which, of course, made our sour grapes taste all the better. We'd see other kids go by sporting Herb's finery and we'd laugh up our sleeves. We even had a mysterious but satisfying epitaph to hurl at them now: "Suckers!"

Then we got it. Davy would take matters into his own hands. He'd hunt down, kill, and skin out a raccoon to fashion his own cap. So would we. The very next day, we headed off to the Ninth Street woods on the south side of town, with murderous intent. We were perfectly armed for the task. We brought peanut butter and jelly sandwiches and a shovel and a Daisy BB gun and a grocery bag. What else could we possibly need? Once the hole was dug and the remains of our sandwiches placed in it for bait, there was little left to do but hide in the nearby bushes and wait for peanut-hungry, unsuspecting coons to enter our trap. Then we'd lower a brush lid onto the pit by the rope we'd strung up in a nearby tree and shoot the bejabbers out of them with the Daisy. It was so simple, yet so brilliant, we were unable to quit congratulating ourselves. As if the coons were already caught and killed, we began to talk knowledgably about the best ways to skin and fashion the hats.

"I say leave some guts hanging down somewhere—so everyone will know we caught 'em."

"Oh yeah. I love that! No one's gonna mistake our caps for sissy hats from Herb's."

"Right, right! The 'suckers!'"

After the second week, we began to get suspicious that maybe we weren't using the right bait after all. Steve then pulled out a brilliant piece of knowledge from, well I don't know where he got it, but since later it actually proved to be accurate, it certainly wasn't original with him.

He said it was a well-known fact that Davy had been in just this situation (this part was a lie, but it was in good context) and had trapped his own coon, just as we were attempting to do (also a lie) by using one of their favorite foods as bait: crawdads (this was the actual keeper of the bunch).

We loved to catch crawdads for the sporting purpose of watching them fight one another, or just to use in the conventional manner of placing them in unusual and highly unsuspected places for other peoples' benefit.

That morning we dug the pit extra deep—in case the scent of clamoring crawdads inflamed the coons into a veritable stampede—set the trap lid, loaded the Daisy, and settled down for what promised to be easy pickins.

"Like shearin' sheep in a barrel," I said knowingly.

"What's that mean?"

"You don't know? Man, if you don't know that you're just a sucker."

"I know what it means all right. I just wanted to see if you knew."

"Well of course I know. I'm the one that said it."

"Right. Right."

After a week we were about as mad as anyone could be. Here's why: We stood watch vigilantly all day long, every day. And no coons came. Then, at night, while we were at home, somebody came and maliciously stole all the crawdads we'd caught and left in the hole. Even tore them apart—just left the claws. It was a mess. They couldn't have done worse if they'd been eating them.

"Hey," I asked, "whoever they are—You s'pose they watch us? I mean like, maybe they're hiding here somewhere in the woods, just laughing at us. Then, when we go home, they come over here and mess up all our crawdads?"

"Yep. I bet that's it. We might as well give up on this. Besides, we've caught all the crawdads worth catching for a mile up and down the creek."

We were pretty shot down by it all. By day the coons were being totally uncooperative. At night unidentified "suckers" were evidently getting thrills decimating our crawdads. As the days of summer flowed away from us, we never suspected our true difficulties actually lay in our own barrel of ignorance, a barrel just filled to overflowing.

Capless, we emerged from the woods. I climbed onto the trailing seat of Steve's twenty-six-inch Huffy with the fat boy tires, and we started the long gradual ascent up the Ninth Street hill. It was hot enough to make the bubbles of tarry asphalt pop satisfyingly beneath the tires.

In the distance we heard a faint rumble. A Golden Guernsey Dairy truck came into sight. The road was narrow, a two-lane asphalt job, so we got off to the side and into the edge of the woods, waiting for it to pass. Maybe ice cream would fall out the back of the truck—chocolate, probably. Who could say? To us that seemed not only possible, but likely. Fair, even.

What happened instead led to everything that followed, and I blame those events on that particular moment. It's stuck with me, not only as a sign of possible intention to the universe, but also that the intentions might be less like "good" and more like "ambiguous."

Yes, in the just universe of a kid's imagination, ice cream would indeed have bounced out the back of the dairy truck. But in the actual universe we were delivered a possum instead. It emerged from the woods with a plan to cross the road (I am second-guessing a possum here)—just as the dairy truck came barreling down the hill. About midroad the possum detected the oncoming truck and went into defensive action: It played dead. This proved less than useful, for two seconds later, it really was dead. The truck drove on, its driver oblivious.

"Cool!" said Steve. "Let's go look at him."

"He's hardly squished or anything."

"No kidding! He's as good as new. Except he's dead."

"Yeah. Still warm and everything."

Steve then assumed the quiet, thoughtful pose I later came to understand meant trouble. Then he spoke the fateful words again: "What would Davy do?"

We reasoned it all out logically. If coons weren't available, and a suicidal possum placed himself at Davy's feet, would Davy look down his snoot at what nature gave him? No sir. Davy would make good use of that critter. We resolved to do the same.

We put the possum in the grocery bag, folded down the top, and hid it in a bucket my dad used to wash the car with, a bucket that always lived on a certain shelf in the garage. I figured nobody would go in there for a while, at least not until we could get together again on Sunday but things came up and it was the following Wednesday before we could have a go at it. By then the possum had "changed." His size was now such that he completely filled the bucket—and could not, in fact, be removed from it.

We went behind the garage to continue the quest to extract him from the bucket without parental interference. His swollen face looked like a great exaggeration of some emotion. Perhaps a smile? I got the notion he was enjoying our difficulties.

"Is he smiling?"

"Naw. Looks more like when you get bad gas."

We had no idea how true that really was. Yet.

After all attempts to pull him out failed, Steve brought physics into the equation. Steve loved to talk like what he thought a scientist would sound like.

"There's a pressure lock problem."

"What's that?"

"You know when you stick your tongue in an empty Coke bottle?"

"Oh, yeah."

"—and suck air so hard your tongue gets locked in there and you have to break the bottle?"

"Sure," I lied. "I've done that before."

"Well, it's just like that. He won't come out unless we reverse the pressure."

"Right."

"Right."

". . . But how do we do that?"

"I hold the bucket sideways. You smack the bottom real hard with a baseball bat. Reverse pressure'll pop him out like a cork."

Like a cannon was more accurate. The possum flew out and—free of any constriction—expanded to his actual (and near totally gaseous) size. Into my dad's tomato plants he rolled faster than a beach ball on a windy day.

"Get 'im quick before someone sees!"

The possum's face now had the definite look of someone suffering from a great pressure of some sort.

"Man, he smells really bad."
"No kidding. We're gonna have to clean that bucket real good."
"Now what?"
"Got to skin him out."
"Right. I'll get a knife."

I tried our table knives for a while, but it was all in vain. Though I struggled I made no headway—instead the face and eyes just bulged out at me. Steve delivered an impressive scientific explanation as to how sawing motions were always used in situations like this and then retrieved his mother's bread knife for the purpose. Then he began sawing.

It worked so well that most our work in "gutting" the animal was done for us when the explosion occurred. Right away the possum's face looked a lot better. More relaxed. My dad's garage, on the other hand, looked a lot worse.

"Oh man! Look! That was great!"
"Yeah! But hey—don't leave 'til it's all cleaned off, OK? You gotta help."
"Right."

Soon we were ready for the next step: shaping and fashioning the possum to take on the form of a human head.

"What about Kevin? We could put it on him."
"My little brother? He'd tell. Remember last time? He loves to get me in trouble."
"Right."

That's when I thought about my mom's bowling ball. She wasn't bowling in the summer league due to a foot operation on her boogered-up toes. A bowling ball seemed like just the right size and shape. I pointed out that it had the additional advantage of being kept in her bowling bag, and thus out of sight.

"Plus," said Steve, "it's got a zipper. With the zipper zipped all the smell will be trapped inside. So nobody'll ever know. When we take it out we'll clean it with perfume or Lysol or something. This is gonna be perfect."

"How long do we leave it 'til the shape holds for good?"

"A fortnight." Steve was a great one for the mysterious terminology. It was a quality I admired about him and one which actually served him well later in life when he entered the pre-owned car business.

"Who gets to wear it first?"

"You can have first go—but only for a day. Then it's my turn, OK?"

"Sure. Man oh man, people aren't gonna believe this, are they?"

"Wait till they see the tail! They're all gonna want one. They're gonna ask: Where can we buy one too?"

"Right. And we'll just smile and say: There's no store in the world gonna sell you one of these. Something like this just can't be bought. Suckers!"

Margarete was our neighbor, two houses down, and she bowled in the summer league. When she realized my mom wasn't going to be using her sparkling new Brunswick ball that summer, she asked if she could borrow it. She knew from previous use that it fit her hand. And she harbored the notion that something about that ball would lift her above her usual average. She couldn't say what it was, but there just seemed to be something special about that ball. My mom was glad to oblige.

I found out about the loan two days before the date Steve and I had set to remove the possum from its lair. It happened like this: About 7:30 that evening, a man came to our door and my mom went outside to talk with him. We were eating TV dinners and watching a western, *Gunsmoke* maybe. The man left, and my mom asked would I like to come into the bedroom a minute, she had something to ask me about. I got a bad feeling right away. Kids just know. I wasn't sure what I had done yet, but I was already exuding guilt mightily.

"Margarete went bowling tonight."

This registered nothing to me. I stalled.

"Uh-huh. I didn't do it on purpose. It was an accident." These were stock replies and you always said them first, regardless of the situation, even if you had no idea what your offense was, which I didn't. I was trying to remember what I had probably broken at their house.

"Well, can you tell me how it got there?"

"It was already there. Probably."

"But you just said you did it."

"Accidentally!"

"Accidentally? How could that happen by accident?! I'm getting mad, buster!"

I could see that. I had to tread carefully. In a situation like this, it never paid to reveal too much. There could be things you'd done which hadn't even been detected yet—and if you said too much you might make things even worse. Better stick to broad generalities.

"Mom—look. Things like this happen all the time."

"They do, huh?"

"Sure. I bet you did the same thing when you were my age. Weren't you ever a kid?" That was a really good line that I got from Steve. He said it worked like magic when used at the right moment. Softened the hardest heart. My mom did not look softened.

"You bet that I—!! Go get the belt!"

I was shocked! My best work was backfiring on me! In desperation I resorted to using specifics.

"Mom! Wait! Really—it was an accident! I didn't mean to break it."

"Break it? Break what?"

Dirty pool! She was asking me to commit to a specific item. Maybe she didn't really know about any broken item after all!

"Look, Mom. I think there's some confusion about all this."

"There certainly is. I'm confused about why Margarete's bowling league was canceled this evening. I'm confused about why the entire bowling alley had to be evacuated."

"Mom, help me understand what it is I did wrong so I can admit it or not."

"I'll help you if you'll help me. For instance: Help me understand how a possum cut himself open and took out his insides—most of his insides—and stretched himself over my bowling ball and then, somehow, zipped himself up inside my bowling bag. Help me understand that."

Remarkably, when Steve and I compared notes afterward, we found we'd each used much the same approach. We'd both asked ourselves the fateful question: What would Davy do? In answer we both came up with whoppers that would've made Crockett himself blush. Mine was along the lines of having seen a very depressed looking possum hanging around our garage in weeks past. Carrying a knife.

In adulthood, I learned the real Crockett was a man of mixed qualities—an ambiguous fellow. The old Disney movie showed Davy going down in glory, swinging Old Betsy at the attacking forces of Santa Ana. In reality, he was among a small group taken alive. Likely he tried to talk his way out of the predicament, but he failed. Like him, I, too, met my Alamo. Unlike him, I lived to prevaricate another day.

Weeks later, Steve and I commiserated. We hadn't got any coons. We hadn't got a cap. We hadn't gotten any glory or fame. Nothing had turned out the way we'd planned.

"Yeah," said Steve, "but we got something really great after all."

"Oh yeah? Name one thing."

"We got a great story."

"Right."

"Right."

"But no one'll believe us."

"Sure they will. Could a kid make up something like that?"

"But what if they don't?"

"Then they're just—"

"—suckers."

"Right."

"Right."

Bob Sander

Bob Sander is a fourth-generation resident of Indianapolis, Indiana, the city where his German American ancestors arrived after the Civil War. Sander remains in the Hoosier capital because, for better and for worse, the fabric of all his life stories is woven there. He's like a square of a quilt now and content to be so. While Sander loves (and tells) stories from elsewhere in the form of folktales, more and more he gravitates toward tales from his life that are all totally true, or should be. A vegetarian, he hunts and consumes mostly humor. For more information visit www.bobsander.com or contact him at sandertales@aol.com.

BICYCLE RACE

Bill Harley

My father was the king of laissez-faire parenting. As a boy, I had free rein to nearly kill myself in myriad ways, as long as he was allowed to comment on my behavior. One of my clearest memories of growing up is of my father sitting on the couch in the living room in the hour before dinner. He would have just gotten home from his job at a publishing company. Armed with a martini and the television playing network news, he would read the *Indianapolis Times*. I would come in from playing and complain about something that had gone wrong that day. I was, unfortunately, an inveterate whiner. The newspaper would lower an inch or two, so I could see his reading glasses over the top of it, and he would say, "Well, that will teach you a lesson."

This pronouncement would send me scurrying from the living room. I never bothered to ask what the lesson was. Who wanted a lecture? Sometimes the lesson was obvious. When I had been hit by a friend because we were playfully throwing rocks toward each other, the lesson was clear: find new friends. Still, it was an annoying, I-told-you-so approach to imparting wisdom. I would bite my tongue and leave the room.

I wasn't surprised, then, when somebody else should have learned the lesson, too. The day after my ninth Christmas, I found a new stopwatch in the parking lot of the hobby shop in Broad Ripple. After no one in the hobby shop claimed it, I took it home and showed it to my father.

> "Look what some kid lost in the parking lot." I said, "He must have just gotten it."
>
> "Well, that will teach him a lesson," my dad observed.

Again, I didn't ask, although it wasn't clear at all what the lesson was, except that life could be pretty crummy sometimes, even on the day after Christmas.

But now the stopwatch was mine. It was a serious tool. With a stopwatch, I had a way to divide time. Today, with digital watches everywhere we look, that doesn't seem very earthshaking, but back then it was—it was an entrée into the adult world. A child's life was really an analog fabric—seamless and flowing. The adult world was divided up into little bits, and so my discovery was an initiation into this world that I was, sadly, all too eager to enter.

I took the stopwatch across the street to my friend Angie Swenson. Angie was a tomboy of truly stunning demeanor—as willing to clothesline tackle anybody in a pickup football game as the meanest cornerback in the NFL. Angie took one look at the stopwatch and said, "We gotta have a race."

She was right. Because we lived in Indianapolis, the interest in the division of time into little bits was expressed in a certain way—it meant we could time ourselves on our bikes, like the drivers did at the Indianapolis Motor Speedway.

The Indianapolis 500 was inescapable. Back then, the only exciting thing that ever happened in Indianapolis took place in the month of May. We lived for the thirty days leading up to Memorial Day, and we all had our favorite drivers. My hero was Parnelli Jones, about whom I knew little except that his mother had given him a name much cooler than mine and that he drove a big red-orange turbine car, number "99," for Andy Granatelli, the president of STP motor products.

Now I know that STP is really something that is used on cars that are on their last legs. If you have a 1988 Monte Carlo, it lives on a quart-a-day diet of STP. Ever notice the blue smoke coming out the exhaust pipe of any junker? It's partially combusted STP. But when the portly Mr. Granatelli came on the television and said that his product was used in all high-performance vehicles, I took it as gospel. I couldn't understand why my father wouldn't put it in his little Fiat. I never asked; I didn't want a lecture.

Word spread through the neighborhood about my stopwatch; kids showed up at the door, asking to see it. Kids I never talked to were suddenly friendly to me. Even Todd Layton, my sworn enemy, asked if he could be in the race. We planned our own version of the 500, to be held the day preceding the race at the Old Brickyard. At the end of Sherwood Drive, where it teed onto Williams Creek Parkway, there was a little triangle of grass. The pavement around it was our racetrack. On the first of May, we got out notebook paper and pencil and began qualifications to determine starting position in our race. We had pit crews with tools taken from basements, garages, and parents' tool chests. We swept the sand from the turns with push brooms. We took apart our bikes, discarding unneeded reflectors and fenders, turning handlebars around and upside down, and experimented with the removal of coaster brakes. I painted the number "99" on my seat and frame and bought a quart of STP at the local hardware store to use the day of the race.

That month, every daylight hour out of school was spent at the track. I was the master of the stopwatch, and we pared seconds off our times, looking for any advantage.

This all may sound a little dangerous, especially considering the noticeable lack of safety equipment on our bikes or selves. But the adults, all practicing the laissez-faire philosophy, considered this endeavor an improvement over the ramps we had constructed in the middle of the street. The day my friends' parents found their preschoolers lying in the street, acting as a barrel as we flew over them on our bikes, the boards of plywood were confiscated. So were the preschoolers.

"What do you think you're doing?" they asked.
"Playing!" we answered. "They liked lying there!"
I complained to my father. "We weren't going to hurt them!"
"That will teach you a lesson," he taught.

Compared to our circus act, the adults looked on the race as an honorable activity.

Then things got even more serious. One day, while we were taking turns circling the track, Mr. Whittier came up the street with a box under his arm. We all stopped and waited for him to arrive, bowing as he reached us. Mr. Whittier was our hero—he was a candy distributor who lived around the corner. Some of my friends had three Halloween costumes so they could just keep going back to his house and gather loot on that sacred night. Mr. Whittier was shaped like a basketball—the proper shape for a candy distributor.

"I brought you kids some candy for the winner of the race," he said, and handed Angie a full box of Hershey candy bars. This was a prize of immeasurable proportions.

"Thanks," we all said at once. We fought over who would take care of the box of candy. Scott Truesdale, the oldest racer at fourteen, took it home and put it in his freezer. We went over and looked at it every day.

Now kids were regularly peering over my shoulder at the stopwatch to make sure I was reading the time correctly. Participation increased. Every kid in the neighborhood raced around the circle, including the Kerrigan twins.

Brucie and Johnny Kerrigan had just turned six years old and had one twenty-inch bike between them. The Kerrigan twins were famous in the neighborhood for their destruction of babysitters. They were the Tartar horde sweeping across the neighborhood in two forty-five-pound bodies. Things mysteriously broke whenever they were in the vicinity. Other children seemed to get hurt by just being around them. No one would babysit for them. Their parents never got to go out. Any Catholic family that has only one set of six-year-old twins has a story to tell about the challenges of parenting. One father, watching them walk by, said aloud to no one, "Twins—the best birth control device on the market."

With only one bike between them, we let the Kerrigans act as a tag team and laughed at their little legs pedaling furiously, the streamers flying from their handlebars, and the playing cards stuck in their spokes. No candy bars for them.

The day of the race came. That morning, I emptied half of the can of STP onto my chain. It had the viscosity of maple syrup at thirty-three degrees Fahrenheit. It was hard to see how something so sticky could make my bike go faster, but I believed in Parnelli Jones and Andy Granatelli.

At the track, we had a full complement of bicycles lined up—twenty-one kids, aged from five to fourteen, riding bikes on training wheels and Schwinn ten-speed racers, lined up three abreast, in a phalanx that extended halfway around the track. The adults surrounded the track, interested in the carnage about to ensue. The Hershey candy bars were displayed on a TV tray in the grass triangle. My brother, smarter than the rest of us, had volunteered to be the pace bike, leading us around the track on his three-speed English racer as we built up speed.

Two important elements determined the nature of the catastrophe that occurred. First, we decided, in a fit of attempted realism, to actually circle the track two hundred times, guaranteeing dizziness, nausea, and confusion for all involved, both participant and observer. It also insured that a lot of participants would not finish because of exhaustion or boredom. Riding a bike loses a lot of its glamour when you ride it in circles for two hours.

Second, I realized at the last minute that we needed someone to count the laps. I had a clipboard with a piece of paper that held every racer's name, but no one to keep track of the different riders. I looked around for a likely accountant. The adults could not be trusted—they were sure to mess things up. The only possibility was whichever Kerrigan twin wasn't racing on the bike at the particular time. I took the clipboard over to the two boys.

"Brucie, Johnny, listen," I said, "you guys take this clipboard and mark down by a person's name every time they go around the racetrack."

"Okay!" they nodded enthusiastically.

"It's really important!" I said.

"Okay!" they said.

It was an impossible task. It would have been impossible for anyone, but it was particularly impossible for the Kerrigan twins. No matter—the impossible seemed like a wonderful thing to them. It never entered their heads that they couldn't do it. In an effort to impress the seriousness of the task upon them, I also handed them my stopwatch.

"You can see how long the race takes," I said.

They immediately started to fight over it.

"Which button do you push?" asked Brucie or Johnny.

"You push one, and let your brother push the other," I said.

"Okay!" they both squealed.

My brother led us around the track twice. The first time around was almost stately, in an eight-year-old kind of way. Parents waved, riders waved back. Cameras clicked. Kids rang bells and honked horns. I saw my father standing by one of the turns, his arms folded, observing. We all stayed in position. The second time around, my brother began to pick up speed, and the formation began to fray. People started to yell at each other.

"Get back where you belong!"

"That's my place!"

"No passing!"

One of the Kerrigans, we could never tell which one, began to pedal furiously, passing other riders before the race began. As my brother pulled off the track and the race began, the Kerrigan in question cut across somebody's path, just missing him, but acting as a catalyst for an accident of gigantic proportions. Riders skidded and slipped in the sand. Bikes entangled. Knees scraped and bled. Parents waded out among the slaughter to extract their children from the pileup.

I went down, too. I scraped the side of my leg and my knee. But I was determined to win, so pulled my bike out of the morass and hopped on it, only to find that the chain had slipped off the sprocket. I got off the bike and tried to get it back on. The STP was gummy and gritty, and by the time I got the chain back on, my hands and forearms were covered in the stuff.

We circled and circled—I lost track of which side of the triangle I was on—the faces on the edge blurred and shifted. The only sounds that entered my consciousness were the squeak of my pedals and the sound of one Kerrigan yelling to the other, "Twenty-five! Twenty-five! . . . Twenty-six! Twenty-six!" I tried to keep track of my circling, but it was hard to know where I was. After fifteen minutes of pedaling, I yelled to one of the Kerrigans, "How many laps have I gone?" "What?" he responded the next time around. The third time around I yelled again, "How many laps have I gone?" On the fourth chance, I was expecting a reply, but the other Kerrigan twin had taken his place. I had to repeat the question six or seven times before I got an answer. "Nine" one of the twins answered authoritatively.

That was impossible. Everything was impossible. I wasn't the only one frustrated. All the other contestants were yelling at the Kerrigans, but the only thing the twins were sure of was how many laps they had completed as a tag team. The race droned on. Riders got bored and quit. It was hot. Fathers wandered off. Scott, the fourteen-year-old and heavy favorite, accidentally ran a seven-year-old girl off the track and retired, overcome by guilt.

As I pedaled on and on, the half quart of STP I had poured up and down the chain began to defy the law of gravity and work its way up the seat stem, onto my legs, shorts, shirt arms, eyes, and hair. It got hotter. I got stickier. It stopped being fun.

"One hundred and forty-nine!" squealed Brucie or Johnny Kerrigan.

That was impossible. Like I said, everything was impossible.

I protested on each lap, and so did the other serious competitors, but there was no judge available to hear the case. Somewhere in an exchange of the Kerrigan bicycle, my stopwatch was dropped and I rode over it. I remember the crunch. I kept riding with tears in my eyes. I rode standing up, my rear end and insides of my legs red and raw from the plastic seat on my bike.

And then, suddenly, mysteriously, Todd Layton, my sworn enemy, held his hand up. "Two hundred!" he yelled. "I win!"

Who knew? Who could tell? We all immediately got off our bikes, claiming that we had completed two hundred laps long ago and were just riding victory laps. The Kerrigans kept circling, racing in a world of their own. A half dozen of us argued in the infield about who deserved the candy bars. Some parent with no sense of the subtleties of juvenile justice decided everyone should get a candy bar.

"No!" we said. "Not that! Anything but that!"

But it was too late—we had complained too loudly and the parents got involved. Kids who hadn't even been in the race were given whole Hershey bars. Mine was melted. After I opened it with my sticky STP-drenched fingers, it had the taste of a petroleum product.

I was beside myself. It couldn't have ended worse. Unable to ride, I walked my bike down the street toward home. My dad had been waiting for me, and without a word joined me, walking beside me, his hand resting lightly on my shoulder to let me know he was there. But the storm was brewing within me, and finally I exploded.

"What a dumb race! Todd Layton says he won and he didn't, and I got knocked off my bike and my stopwatch broke, and the Kerrigans can't count and this STP got all over me and kids who didn't deserve them got candy bars. The whole race was ruined! It stinks!"

We walked another six or seven paces, and then my dad said it. "Well, that will teach you a lesson."

I was flabbergasted. How could he say that to me? We walked down the street as I thought about this. What lesson could possibly be learned from this debacle? The injustice was staggering. And finally, I couldn't help myself. After all these years of not asking, avoiding the full-barreled lecture that was bound to ensue, I finally wanted to know. I didn't care if I got a lecture.

"What lesson is that?" I asked. "What am I supposed to learn?"

We walked a little farther as I waited for the answer, and then my father shrugged his shoulders and said, "Oh, I don't know."

I stopped in the street and looked at him. What? He didn't know? That was it? That was the lesson I'd been avoiding all these years? He didn't know? I waited for more, but none was forthcoming.

I walked behind him all the way home. We got back in the house, and I went in my bedroom and stripped off my clothes. I sat on my bed in my underwear and thought about the race and my father's words. They were like a Zen koan. "I don't know," I repeated to myself over and over again, trying to see the wisdom embedded in the comment. It was immutable. Impenetrable.

And then it hit me. My father was telling me that there was a lesson to be learned, but that it was up for me to decide what it was. No one else could tell me what life meant. I had to decide myself. It was pure genius—the ultimate in laissez-faire parenting—terrifying and liberating at the same time. I should draw my own lessons from the stupid things I did.

Suddenly, I knew what lesson there was to be learned from the bike race. Maybe there were many, but one in particular stood out. It is a lesson I learned that day, and I have never forgotten it—a rule that I follow to this day.

I have never put STP Oil Treatment on or in anything I own. I never will.

Bill Harley

Bill Harley's original work combines song and story to paint a vibrant, humorous, and meaningful portrait of American life. One of the finest performers for families in the country, he has also authored several plays and children's books. Harley is a regular contributor to public radio programs, including commentaries on NPR's All Things Considered *and as host of Vermont Public Radio's* Camel's Hump Radio. *His venues include kindergarten classrooms, teacher conferences, and concert stages with symphony orchestras. His recordings for children, families, and adults have garnered numerous national awards, including a Grammy Award. For more information visit www.billharley.com/.*

SOME ENCHANTED WEDNESDAY

Syd Lieberman

I loved musicals when I was growing up in the 1950s. It was the golden age for movie musicals: *Oklahoma, Singin' in the Rain, Pajama Game, The King and I, My Fair Lady, Guys and Dolls, South Pacific.* The list goes on and on. Now it may sound odd to some of you that a little boy would love musicals, but I had my reasons. First, I was in love with love, and musicals are all about love.

In first grade, I fell in love with my teacher Miss Arkis. I was so in love with her that one day when the class got out of control, I sat perfectly still with my hands folded on my desk hoping she would see me and notice. She did. And she let me paint later in the day when everyone else had to do work. I was crushed when I found out she was getting married.

But I got over it and in second grade fell in love with a girl my own age. I was so in love with Elyse Auslander that I used to sneak out after dinner, walk the block to where she lived, and stand outside her apartment building gazing at her third-floor windows. I was a seven-year-old Romeo, hoping for a glimpse of her, but really I didn't even need it. I just felt good knowing she was up there. One winter night as I stood staring up under the little cone of light cast by one of the old-fashioned streetlights, the snow began to gently fall. I was so overcome by the moment that I began singing "Silent Night."

And musicals are also filled with happy endings. I kept wanting and expecting real-life happy endings as a kid, but they were hard to come by.

One beautiful, warm spring day—a day on which all the flowers and trees began to bud, a day in which you could smell the end of school—Tony Mortello and I burst out of our second-grade classroom to run all the way home for lunch. We must have noticed the tree before, but suddenly it was as if we were seeing it for the first time, as if it had just been planted for us. We stopped and smiled at one another. There was no question that we had to climb the tree, and so up we went, from branch to branch, and then we swung out, let go, and hit the pavement running.

When we got back to school after lunch, our names were on the blackboard. I was sure I was going to get some award. I didn't know what I had done to deserve it, but I was sure I had done something. I sat there beaming when my teacher came in the room. She pointed at our names on the blackboard and shouted, "You two have been seen climbing one of our school's trees. Get down to Mrs. Corilla this instant."

It was as if I had been hit by lightning. Not only wasn't I going to be honored, but I had to go to the office of our assistant principal. The older kids called her Corilla the Gorilla. But she was nothing like a gorilla.

She wore black and she was thin: thin body, thin face, thin lips, thin nose, thin eyes. Her room was cold and dark. All the shades were drawn, and she had a black curtain that she pulled across them. Corilla was seated at her desk, and with a finger, she motioned me in. I stood in front of her, waiting, but she didn't say anything. She just sat there staring at me. Just staring at me. I was only seven and completely terrified. I wanted to run out but I seemed rooted to the floor. Finally, I couldn't stand it any longer and I burst into tears, confessing my sin and promising never to climb a school tree again. It was like appearing before the Spanish Inquisition. "Make sure you keep that promise," she said and then she dismissed me.

But that was nothing compared to what happened to me in third grade. One day we were coloring pie plates for an open house. We were going to hang them up for our mothers to see. Well, I'm color blind but I didn't know that in third grade. I used to read the names of the colors off the crayons to see what they were. I thought all the kids did that.

It was a gloomy, rainy afternoon, but somehow that made the room seem cozier: a little island of warm light in the midst of darkness. There I was coloring away with all my seven-year-old heart and soul. I was the first one finished and I was so happy with what I had done that I rushed up to my teacher, Miss Riglander—she must have been 105—and shoved my pie plate under her nose as she worked at her desk. "Miss Riglander, Miss Riglander," I shouted, "Look at my pie plate. Look at my pie plate."

And she said loud enough for everyone in the class to hear: "This is the ugliest pie plate I've ever seen and I won't hang it up." Do you believe that? Do you believe she did that to a seven-year-old? It was as if she took a knife to me.

Well, of course, all the kids rushed over to see it. My last memory of that day is me sitting on my pie plate and crying as all the kids crowded around my desk.

So you can see why I liked musicals. They had happy endings. Endings filled with love—astonishing endings where love occurs between a poor flower girl and a professor, a Salvation Army worker and gambler, a nurse and rich planter, a teacher and a King. The bad guys lose, the good guys win, and everything is so wonderful that people can't help but burst into song.

Oklahoma, where the wind comes sweepin' down the plain
And the wavin' wheat can sure smell sweet
When the wind comes right behind the rain.
Oklahoma, ev'ry night my honey lamb and I
Sit alone and talk and watch a hawk
Makin' lazy circles in the sky.
(Oklahoma)

I know a dark secluded place.
A place where no one knows your face.
A glass of wine, a fast embrace.
It's called . . . Hernando's Hideaway . . . OLÉ
(Pajama Game)

Hello young lovers, whoever you are,
I hope your troubles are few.
All my good wishes go with you tonight,
I've been in love like you.
(The King and I)

We've got sunlight on the sand.
We've got moonlight on the sea.
We've got mangoes and bananas
We can pick right off the tree,
We've got volleyball and ping-pong
And a lot of dandy games!
What ain't we got?
We ain't got dames!
(South Pacific)

Luck be a lady tonight,
Luck be a lady tonight,
Luck if you've ever been a lady to begin with
Luck be a lady tonight.
(Guys and Dolls)

I'm singin' in the rain
Just singin' in the rain.
What a glorious feelin'.
I'm happy again . . .
I walk down the lane
With a happy refrain,
Just singin', singin' in the rain.
(Singin' in the Rain)

By the time I was eleven, I no longer had crushes on teachers and I had gotten over my second-grade sweetheart. I had a new love: baseball. And when I was eleven years old, I decided that I wanted to collect autographs of baseball players. I even bought a brown autograph book to put them in. "Autographs" was written in gold on the cover. I don't know why I wanted them. None of my friends had autographs, and until then, I had been satisfied with collecting baseball cards. TOPPS was the brand. Their packages cost a nickel and held about five cards and a thin, flat, rectangular slice of pink bubble gum. I'd buy five packs for a quarter, stuff all that gum in my mouth, chomp away and head to a friend's house. There my buddies and I would spread our collections out on the floor and begin wheeling and dealing, hoping to get lucky.

Lucky to me was getting pictures of Cubs. They were my team. I identified with them. The Cubs do not have happy endings. They haven't won the World Series since 1905 and haven't been in one since 1945. In the 1950s when I was growing up, they never finished higher than fifth in an eight-team league. In that decade, they never even made it into the first division. The players must have felt as if they were entering Dante's Inferno when they came to the Cubs: "Abandon all hope ye who enter here." Eddie Miksis, Roy Smalley, Dee Fondy, Randy Jackson. The list of losing players goes on and on and on year after year after year. Hal Jeffcoat, Hank Sauer, Harry Chiti. Harry Chiti was a catcher. I was at a game once where the Cubs were winning by one run in the ninth. The Cardinals had the bases loaded and two out and the batter hit a pop foul. Chiti tosses off his mask, pounds his mitt, and camps under it. The Cubs are going to win. Not only did he miss it. The ball hit him right in the head. On the next pitch, the batter singled, two runs scored, and the Cubs went on to lose.

But it didn't matter to me that the Cubs were losers. They were my team, and, anyway, hope sprung eternal within this little breast.

The problem was that I couldn't get any Cubs' autographs. After the game, I would wait under the stands where the Cubs would exit from their locker room to get into their cars and drive home. They'd begin to come out and like everyone I'd wave my scorecard in the air but there were always so many people, and I was usually in the back. I was a little eleven-year-old, and I don't think a Cub ever saw me.

By late August my empty autograph book sat on my desk, a reproach. I could hear it pleading, "Fill me, Fill me." So I decided that if I couldn't get the Cubs' autographs at least I would get their opponents'. The Milwaukee Braves were in town, and they were a good team. They had Hank Aaron and Eddie Mathews. They finished second that year.

I went to the game not only filled with hope but also with a plan. I left the game in the seventh inning and took up a spot next to the Braves' bus parked outside the ballpark on Addison. The Braves would take this bus back to their hotel after the game. I positioned myself right next to the bus's door and under the first window. I figured I'd get a few autographs as the Braves walked by me, and I was sure to get the autograph of the guy sitting in the window above me.

When the game ended, a big crowd began to gather by the bus, but I wasn't worried. With my spot, I was sitting in the catbird seat. And then the Braves started to leave their dressing room. They quickly cut a thin line through the crowd, as people yelled and pushed scorecards at them. They had lost, and not many wanted to stop and give autographs. And as they hurried to the bus, the crowd began to rush after them. They looked like a wave of people, a wave rushing right at me. They slammed me into the side of the bus and pinned me there as they pushed their scorecards up at the Braves. It was horrible. Not only wasn't I getting any autographs, it was scary. No one seemed to care that a small kid was being crushed.

I don't know how long this went on—it seemed like an eternity—and then the crowd thinned out and left. I stood there, staring sadly at my empty scorecard when I heard a voice above me say, "You been there the whole time, kid?" I looked up at a black ballplayer in the window above me.

"Yeah," I said.

"Well, give me that scorecard." I handed it up, he signed it, and then I heard him say, "Hey, guys, sign this, will you?" And he passed it around the inside of the bus. He looked at me, smiled, and said, "This will take a few minutes." A few minutes! It could have taken a few years. I was going to get all the Braves' autographs. And as I stood there with my mouth open, I realized I was in my own musical.

Sung to the melody of "Some Enchanted Evening"

Some enchanted Wednesday
You may see a stranger,
you may see a stranger
Upon a crowded bus
And you know even then
He's a man among men

(Repeat the melody)
Hank Aaron, Eddie Mathews
Buhl and Spahn and Adcock
Rice and Crowe and Crandell
Scrawled across that crowded card.
And you knew for a fact
When he gave the card back
That you would never forget that man.

George Crowe. He played first base for the Braves that year. He played nine years in the big leagues for three different teams. His lifetime batting average was .270. One year he hit .301. He was on the National League All-Star team in 1958, but he never got into the game. He wasn't really a star. He was a good, sound baseball player. But to a small boy on that Wednesday afternoon, he was the greatest baseball player that ever lived.

Reprise . . .
Hank Aaron, Eddie Mathews

Buhl and Spahn and Adcock
Rice and Crowe and Crandell
Scrawled across that crowded card.
And you knew for a fact
When he gave the card back
That you would never forget that man.

Syd Lieberman

Syd Lieberman is an internationally acclaimed storyteller, an author, and an award-winning teacher. Many of his best-loved stories deal with growing up and raising a family in Chicago. He is also known for his original historical pieces and his signature versions of Jewish and literary tales. Lieberman's work has garnered awards from the American Library Association, Parent's Choice, *and* Storytelling World. *He has taught storytelling at the Kennedy Center and Disney World and received commissions from NASA; the Smithsonian Institution; Johnstown, Pennsylvania; Historic Philadelphia; and the Van Andel Museum Center. For more information, visit www.sydlieberman.com or contact him at slieberman@etpost.net.*

George Crowe, the hero of this story, is a member of the Indiana Baseball Hall of Fame.

THE MAN WHO PLANTED TREES

Liza Hyatt

In 1966 my parents bought a house on ten acres of land in the town of Zionsville in Boone County, Indiana. At that time, this house was "in the country," with a soybean farm across the street and sheep and cows grazing just down the road. Our house was a small ranch built in the 1950s, painted aqua green, and surrounded by oaks, shagbark hickories, black walnuts, and maples.

The entire wooded ten acres had been mowed by the previous owners. My father, busy owner of Hyatt's Furniture Store, soon learned that it took all Saturday to cut the grass in our yard. He sat atop the riding lawn mower, driving up and down, back and forth, circling around dozens of mature trees. And then all the grass clippings had to be raked up and edges trimmed. By the time that was done, the grass had grown and it was time to mow again.

About half of the ten acres was sectioned off by a fence. My mother, who grew up on a dairy farm in New Jersey, called that area "the pasture," though it looked no different from the rest of the lawn and we grazed no livestock there. My father decided that, though the home owners before us had groomed the lawn as if they were caretakers of a suburban country club, he had no such aspirations. After only a few yard-work weekends, my father never again entered the pasture with a lawn mower. Instead, he let it return to the wild.

The tall grasses and weeds came back first. There were thistle and other prickly plants that burred shoestrings, socks, and Barney the beagle's fur. Ferns began to grow. And wildflowers. There were spring beauties, violets, toothwort, trout lilies, mayapples, jack-in-the-pulpits, and in late summer and early fall, Queen Anne's lace, black-eyed Susans, and ironweed. Blackberry brambles tangled their way into the tall grass at the pasture's edge. I remember picking handfuls of small, purple berries and dropping them into my cereal bowl on early summer mornings.

The animals returned as well, squirrels, chipmunks, rabbits, and raccoons whose light-reflecting eyes glowed brassy green if caught after dark with the beam of a flashlight. Opossums. A fox or two. Snakes. Frogs. The turtle we discovered slowly lumbering across our driveway. Insects. Chiggers and mosquitoes and ticks. Moths, including the small white ones that swirled around the porch light, and the eerie green luna moth that sat slowly fanning its pale iridescent wings on the front step one summer dusk. Fireflies. Praying mantis. Inchworms. Walking sticks. And birds. The hawk my mother pointed to, circling above our land one morning. Woodpeckers, both downy and palliated. Bobwhites. Cardinals, blue jays, and robins. Screech owls and hoot owls. A whip-poor-will.

And as these wild things came back to the little woods, the oaks and maples continued to drop their acorns and helicopter-blade-seeds called samara. With nothing to mow them down, the acorns and maple samara were able to find a foothold in the wilderness. They nuzzled their way into the dirt, put out roots, shot up green seedling stalks, and began to grow, until dozens of infant trees proliferated around the poison-ivy clad trunks of their parent trees.

I became used to falling asleep on summer nights on the screened porch listening to the forest symphony, picking out the voices of the orchestra. The leaves of the trees whispering in the wind. The drone of the cicadas. The rasp of crickets. The debate of the katydids: "Katy did. Katy didn't." The soprano of spring peepers and the deep bass of bullfrogs. Barney the beagle baying at the moon. The neighbor's collie calling back. Miles down the road, another dog joining the chorus. The hoot owl's rhythmic hoot. And on magical nights, the aria of the whip-poor-will. I grew up believing that on every summer night of my life I would hear such music.

One spring, when I was in third grade, my father learned that he could order large quantities of tree seedlings from the state for very affordable rates. He ordered white pine and tulip poplar in packages of fifty. Intending to convert even more of the ten acres to unmown forest, he ordered three hundred seedlings in all. And that May, he began spending his weekends away from his furniture store planting trees.

My brother, sister, and I ignored him at first. He called what he was doing "working in the yard." And we were not interested in anything called "work," especially not on the weekends or during summer vacation. We had fun things to do. Swimming, Little League, art lessons, building forts and pioneer settlements in the woods, capturing fireflies, searching for arrowheads, writing stories, reading, playing whiffle ball at dusk with ghost men filling the bases.

But one summer Saturday, my father went to town to do something called "building upkeep" at his furniture store and I went with him, not for the "building upkeep," but because I liked drawing pictures in the store office using Magic Markers—those big fat, intoxicating permanent markers that made amazingly loud squeaks when I pulled them back and forth across the paper. While I did this, my father cleaned the gutters around the store. In the rotting leaf pulp compacted there, he found three maple seedlings growing from seeds that had twirled into the gutters. He put these tiny trees into three Styrofoam coffee cups, packed some dirt in around the tender roots, and placed the cups on the backseat of the blue Ford station wagon. We drove home that afternoon singing the song we always sang together, "Zip-ah-dee-do-da, zip-ah-dee-ay. My, oh my, what a wonderful day. . . ."

He set the coffee-cup maples onto his workbench in the garage and brought us kids to them. "There's one for each of you," he explained. "Your very own tree. And if you want, I'll show you how to plant them."

So that afternoon, carrying the tree-filled cups in our hands, we accompanied Dad outside. He said we could pick where we wanted to plant our trees. I wanted to plant mine in the flower bed up against the screened porch where I would hear the sounds of its leaves as the first layer of the forest symphony each dusk. But Dad explained that planting trees too close to the house was not good for the tree or the house and suggested we move it back several feet.

There, he showed us how to dig up a small circle of sod, then dig down a little deeper, making a hole about the size of the jumbo peanut butter jar we trapped fireflies in. We scooped the tree and its dirt out of the coffee cup and placed the tree into the hole, sprinkling more dirt in around the pale, hair-fine roots. When the hole was filled, we packed the soil down by standing on it, pressing our weight into it, being careful not to trample the tender tree. Then we unwound the hose, coil by coil, until it was long enough to reach and we watered the tree, making a frothy brown soup around its flower-stalk thin trunk.

We decided to plant my brother's and sister's trees nearby so that they would grow together as a family. After each of the tiny trees was planted and watered, my father found his camera and asked us each to pose beside our own tree. I said that I felt like a giant towering over an ankle-tall green pixie.

My father laughed. "You just wait," he said. "By the time you are old enough to have kids of your own, that tiny tree will tower over you. And then we will come back here," he promised. "You and your little ones can stand underneath your grown-up tree and I will take another picture. That's how we will measure our lives—by the trees."

Then he said we were done for the day and we could go off and play like we usually did. But my brother said, "This is fun. Can't we plant more trees?" So we followed my father to the garage, helped him load the wheelbarrow with pine and tulip tree seedlings. One of us got to carry the shovel. One of us got to drag the hose. And one of us got to help steer the wheelbarrow. In this way, we went with him to the front yard where he'd already planted at least fifty trees. He told us that someday the house would not be visible from the road because of all the trees. Looking at the knee-high saplings dotting the yard, I didn't believe such a time would ever come.

We helped him plant another ten trees that afternoon, digging up soil, pushing it back in around the sapling's roots, tamping down the soil, making mud soup with the hose to water the saplings. When we were done planting, we took turns riding in the wheelbarrow as my father pushed. He gave us each several rides, and on our last ride dropped us off at the door to the screened porch, telling us to go in and wash up for supper.

Twilight seemed to breathe itself up from roots of the trees as we gathered at the screened-porch table for a supper of our summer favorites—fried chicken, corn on the cob, and watermelon for dessert. We sat outside on the porch step to eat the watermelon and compete to spit the seeds farthest. The fireflies floated from their hiding places in the grass. We ran after them, caught them, and let them go. They left a trace of firefly smell on our palms—slightly metallic and grassy.

Too soon it was time for bed. We set up our cots on the porch, dressed in our lightest pajamas, and slid under cotton sheets, positioning them so they barely covered us because the night was still deliciously warm. To tuck us in, my father read to us.

I closed my eyes and let the story he read conjure pictures in my mind. Pictures of a windy, desolate place in the mountains. Pictures of parched soil and dry streambeds. Of a village of people whose hungry, harsh faces were as parched and pitted as the land around them.

Then the story took me to another place, miles from this village, and I saw an old man, who lived alone, walking slowly through the barren hills, stopping every few feet to dig a hole and plant an acorn taken from the pouch at his side. Every day, the story said, this man planted a hundred acorns.

Then the story painted pictures of exploding bombs, shattered cities, dying soldiers—of World War One and World War Two being fought in places both near and far from the old man and his acorns.

And finally, the story took us back to the old man, still alive and planting trees miles from where he had begun. Many of the first acorns he had planted were now tall, strong trees steadily sowing their own seeds. A forest had sprung up in places where only the most tenacious weeds had once grown. Birds nested in the young trees. Animals made their homes in the new forest. Grass and wildflowers grew in the shade. The many roots, now thickly woven through the dirt, held moisture in. The streambeds flowed with fresh, sweet water. Scientists arrived to study this unprecedented, inexplicable growth of a new forest. In the harsh, hungry village, people were planting gardens. Flowers grew in window boxes. The well was full. Faces were soft with smiles. Children played in the streets. And visitors who came to the village decided to stay because it was such a good place to live.

My father finished reading and sat, silently looking out into the night where the fireflies flickered and the forest symphony was going strong. I looked in the direction of his gaze. The yard was enveloped in darkness. But I knew that he was looking toward—and somehow seeing—the little trees he had planted that summer, some with our help.

He smiled at me and leaned down to tuck the loose sheets under my chin, saying, "Sleep tight. Don't let the bedbugs bite."

My sister Emily asked, "Can we help plant trees again tomorrow?" Dad smiled and answered, "If you want to. But no squabbling or staying up all night. So we can get an early start in the morning."

"Can we plant a hundred trees tomorrow?" I asked. Dad chuckled. "We can't plant quite that many. But just think. What kind of a world would it be if right now, everyone, from here to China and back, were to plant just one tree?"

Then he kissed us on the foreheads and slipped into the house, leaving us to answer his question within our own hearts.

I lay on my cot, my eyes drifting closed, letting the forest symphony lull me to sleep, as I trusted it always would. I heard the leaves of the trees, some planted this day, whispering together. The drone of the locust. The rasp of crickets. The debate of the katydids. Barney the beagle baying at the moon. The neighbor's collie answering. A dog miles away joining the chorus. The hoot owl. And the whip-poor-will, because it was a magic night.

Behind closed eyes, half-awake, half-asleep, I saw a dream image of a man, walking across the world, planting trees. And the man that I saw looked just like my father.

About twenty years later, a book caught my eye at the library. Its title—*The Man Who Planted Trees*, by Jean Giono—reminded me of my father, so I checked it out. Back home in my post-grad school digs in an old Indianapolis apartment building, I opened the book and read, recognizing it immediately as the one my father read to us that summer when I was eight.

When I finished reading, I stepped out on my apartment's tiny balcony and stood looking at the view—the gray sky of early April, a small, treeless square of grass and another brick apartment building. It had been years since I had fallen asleep listening to the forest symphony and more than a decade since the Zionsville house and its ten acres had been sold in the wake of my parents' divorce. It felt as if my life and the world had changed so much in that decade that coming to live again on a quiet country road in a house surrounded by old trees and space to plant more was now an impossible longing. A longing that the chanced-upon book had painfully intensified.

Then, I noticed something growing in the planter I had left on the balcony unattended all winter. Amidst dead stalks of last summer's annuals, there was a hint of green—a tiny volunteer maple seedling. How the seed had managed to find my planter in this treeless place I did not know. But, seeing it, I knew there was something I could do. I dug up the little seedling and transferred it to a Styrofoam cup. And that afternoon, I drove out to visit my old childhood home.

I almost drove past the old place without recognizing it. The pasture had been subdivided and four houses had been built where none existed before. The farm next door had been sold, and a subdivision crowded with new homes was going in. A wide swath of my own yard had been made into the road leading into this development.

Saddened by so much change, I almost talked myself out of what I had planned. But then I saw my old house hidden behind tall pines and tulip poplars, just as my father had hoped. I pulled into my old driveway where we had ridden in the wheelbarrow after planting trees. With my Styrofoam-cup seedling in hand, I knocked on the door of the house. A middle-aged woman answered.

"Hi," I said, hoping the lump in my throat would go away. "I grew up in this house and helped my father plant some of the trees in your yard. I was wondering if I could look around, and, if you don't mind, find a place to plant this little maple seedling."

The woman, who introduced herself as Mrs. Mary Dolan, beamed, delighted to invite me in to "come home" for a little bit. "I bet those are your handprints in the cement out in the garage," she said. She showed me three sets of child-sized hands and a date that had been carved into the cement beneath them. I could not believe my hands had once been that small.

I told her about planting the three maple seedlings and my father saying that we would measure our lives by those trees.

"I think I know which trees those are," she said, leading me around the house toward the screened porch.

There, providing beautiful shade to the old porch, stood three mature maple trees. On one branch someone had hung a hammock swing.

"I come here a lot," Mary Dolan said. "You won't believe this, but I always think of these trees as a little family."

We picked a place nearby and planted the tiny maple seedling I had brought with me. We marked the spot with a stick, and I was promised that the little tree would be protected.

"We hated to sell that land north of the house for the road," Mary Dolan said. "But it was college tuition for our son. And we got them to move it just a hair so that some of the biggest trees were spared. This spring, we are going to plant several new trees in along the fence there to replace the ones that were lost. I'll think of you and your dad while we're at it. You know, we knew your dad. Bought furniture at his store when we first moved to town."

We talked for a while about my dad and his Florida retirement. Then Mrs. Dolan left me alone in the yard to reminisce a while. I sat in the hammock swing and looked up at how tall the three maples had grown. The moment wasn't at all what I had imagined when my father promised I would someday measure my life by those trees. But it felt right to have come back to find our three maples thriving in the midst of a world of constant change, where environmental loss is a constant presence at our own backdoors. And as I sat there, I realized I had found more than the three maples. I had found something every storyteller learns, with each listening and each telling. I had found that stories are the true measure of our lives—the stories we are told by others, the stories we tell ourselves—for it is in our stories that we learn to live on this world. And I was glad that I had given my story to Mary Dolan, who would weave her story and mine together, who would sit in the hammock on summer evenings, listening to the forest symphony rising up from the three maples, from the trees she would plant that spring, from the pines and tulip poplars my father planted (with the help of three children) on that loved, remnant of land in Zionsville.

Liza Hyatt

Liza Hyatt has been a professional storyteller since 1989. She has performed throughout central Indiana at schools, museums, libraries, and festivals. She performs world folktales, historical stories, and personal stories with heroes who become wise by daring to explore community, nature, and creativity. Her love of storytelling originated in childhood. Raised by parents who considered themselves book-loving weirdos in a rural Indiana town, stories were always part of daily life. With bookshelves in every room of the house, Hyatt grew up reading, listening to stories read to her, and began writing her own stories at an early age. For more information visit www.heart-of-art-studio.com or contact her at lizah2@lizahyatt.com.

OLD AUBBEENAUBBEE AND THE MULTIFUNCTION BOY SCOUT KNIFE

George Schricker

It was in the eighteenth century,
In 1761,
A Potawatomi woman,
Gave birth to a strong young son,
The boy was strong and able,
To set his spirit free,
And his mother called him Aubbee,
At the head of the Kankakee

My childhood was haunted by stories my grandfather told me of Indiana's dark past, especially the tales of the Potawatomi leaders, Menominee and Aubbeenaubbee.

I loved hearing about the heroic Menominee, a Potawatomi leader who stood up to the United States government by refusing to sign treaties that would remove his people to lands west of the Mississippi. Menominee was forced at gunpoint to move on, and he accompanied his people to Kansas, helped them along the way, and died there peacefully after the removal.

In contrast to the clearly heroic Menominee, Aubbeenaubbee was a more complex historical figure. Much of his life he fought bravely in battle, but later he succumbed to drunkenness and met a horrible end. So over the years, Aubbeenaubbee slipped from my memory. I did not recall his real significance to my early life until the 1980s, when I wrote a song about him, remembered an important campout, and recalled the significance of my trusty Boy Scout knife.

The "Trail of Death" begins at the Twin Lakes, just three miles from my boyhood home in Plymouth, Indiana. My friends and I would often ride our bikes out to the area to swim or fish, and we would stop at the statue of Menominee, erected there to commemorate that tragic period of Indiana history. We would stare at his proud, peaceful figure, gazing southward from his high limestone pedestal, and try to imagine what it must have been like to live in those times.

"Wouldn't you have loved to have seen this place back then?"

"Why couldn't they just stay here?"

"Why didn't anybody help them stay?"

We all realized that although the Potawatomi had been removed from the area, they had been the ones who knew the most about living off the land here. They had what we young boys all sought so dearly: survival skills.

Growing up in the 1950s and early 1960s, in the midst of the cold war, we boys lived in a state of high alert. We knew all about the atom bomb and that our parents had been encouraged to build basement shelters in case of a nuclear attack. We practiced our drills in school, ducking under our desks, and tucking our heads into our knees. We were fairly certain Armageddon was just around the corner and that the only way to survive it was to be prepared. Who better to prepare us in the art of survival but the natives who had lived off the land for thousands of years before our arrival? Who better to equip us for the trials we were all certain we would soon have to endure?

He learned to hunt with hickory bow,
And long knife at his side,
At ten he put meat on the table,
He wandered far and wide.
He was always greeted kindly,
No matter where he'd go,
He was a friend of all the Indians,
And welcomed in their homes.

Now our vision of native life was informed more by our imaginations rather than facts. We fashioned homemade spears, whittling them with kitchen knives. We ran around shirtless and barefoot, with mud, charcoal, or our moms' lipstick smeared on our faces, yelling as we sprang out at each other from behind bushes. We climbed trees and made forts of sticks and branches. We tried to walk silently and sneak up on our friends. We engaged in tests of strength by wrestling or throwing heavy rocks as far as we could. We made crude bows and arrows and shot them at squirrels, birds, and anything else that moved. Though our missiles fell off target, we knew that, with a bit more practice, we could easily survive in the wild. All in all, we were a fearsome lot. But, most importantly, we felt prepared!

Truthfully, I may have been the one more caught up in this survival idea than my friends, thanks to my circumstances. When I was five, my father had had life-threatening surgery to correct a problem with his aortic valve. As a result, my mother went to work full time and I started kindergarten early. Not more than two years later, my father was back in the hospital facing even riskier surgery on the same aortic valve and, lucky for us, became the first person to survive such an ordeal. All of this filled the household with more than a little anxiety. To make matters worse, my father, once fully recovered, took a job as a traveling salesman in order to retain health insurance coverage. This made me "man of the house" five days a week from the age of seven to thirteen. I faced that burden by searching for survival skills wherever I could find them.

My mother, sensing my anxiety and need for support, suggested I join the Boy Scouts of America. That organization even came complete with the motto: "Be Prepared." I began at the Lion Cub rank in the Cub Scouts. Fortunately, Tom, one of my best friends at the time, was already in the scouts and this made getting involved easy.

One of the things I loved most about scouting was the uniform. I'm sure many of you are familiar with the traditional blue shirt, blue cap, and bright yellow neckerchief. I thought the neckerchief was the neatest part of the whole thing. It was a practical tool in so many ways: tourniquet, signal flag, carryall, slingshot, and, of course, in a dire emergency, handkerchief. Wearing something so useful made me feel well prepared and capable.

As I grew older, I entered the Webelos, where I earned the privilege of carrying a Boy Scout knife and a Boy Scout hatchet. These potentially dangerous items were a sign of real independence and maturity. A knife and a hatchet on your belt during campouts meant that you had earned the right to carry them. It meant that you knew how to use them safely, carefully, and wisely. In other words, it implied that you had been tested! And most importantly, it was manhood that you could wear on your belt.

For me, it also meant that I could defend my sister, my mother, and myself while my dad was on the road.

As soon as Tom and I had acquired all the necessary skills, both of us took the tests and earned the right to acquire our first knife. Shopping for this knife was an extremely important task, especially for me. I spent days walking downtown to the sporting goods store, the dime store, and the hardware store, looking through all the knives in the big glass cases there. There were little ones that easily fit into your pocket, there were big Barlow knives that had two really good blades and sturdy bone handles, and there were sleek red knives that contained multiple tools and a small pair of scissors. All of these were permitted, once you had your knife patch, but none of them was a true Boy Scout knife, and for me this crucial distinction mattered most.

A Boy Scout knife was no ordinary knife. It was a multifunction tool that was truly inspiring. Not only did it have a knife of favorable size, but it also housed a fork, spoon, and can opener. You could open a can of stew, cook it in the can, and eat it with your spoon and fork. For a boy, it was heaven!

I took deliberate care of my knife. I cleaned and oiled it after using it, I whittled away from myself, and I remembered to close the blade as soon as I finished with it. I never played with it. I also learned all the creative things you can do with a properly sharpened knife, like making whistles from reeds, whittling a cooking stick, cutting up food for meals, cutting twine for bindings, and in an emergency, cutting your neckerchief into bandages.

As soon as I got the knife, I began to dream of the belt carrier that went with it. It could be purchased as a do-it-yourself kit, which you sewed together. A few weeks after buying the knife I began sewing it. When it was finished, I proudly wore it "loaded" at my scout meetings.

Tom wasn't quite as fascinated by knives as I was. He bought a small yellow knife that had multiple blades of different sizes and shapes, but he also bought a special green Boy Scout flashlight. The wonderful thing about this flashlight was that instead of shining straight ahead at the end of the tube, it turned a ninety-degree angle. It came equipped with a button at the side that allowed the user to flash the light on and off, so you could send long distance messages in Morse code in emergencies. In another position, the beam would flash on and off automatically, sending a warning signal. Of course, the other neat thing was that it came complete with a clip to wear it on your belt.

So when Tom and I were together at a campout or a meeting, we were a force to be reckoned with. Tom had his multifunction flashlight on his belt, and I had my multifunction knife at my side. Of course we both had our multifunction neckerchiefs, belts, and Cub Scout caps. Together we were a living, breathing, chest-thumping Boy Scout motto in action. We were the essence of Be Prepared. Now, being prepared in Webelos was crucial. We knew from all the stories that we heard, something lay ahead for us that everyone referred to (in whispers) as "The Initiation."

One day when he was thirteen,
On his way to Hickory flats,
The air turned strong and heavy,

Aubbee looked behind his back,
He'd come upon a massacre,
A village of Indian friends,
Got a taste of the white man's vision,
And the death it did portend.

Oh, Aubbeenaubbee,
"One Who Looks Behind,"
You've seen the truth,
In the white man's eyes,
And it's eaten up your mind.
Oh, Aubbeenaubbee,
Caught in-between,
The end of the Indian Nation,
And the beginning of the white man's dream.

When we reached the rank of Tenderfoot Scouts, we discovered that our first overnight campout would take place in May at the Boy Scout reservation on the Twin Lakes, our old stomping grounds. This was the very land that had been occupied by the Potawatomi people not more than 125 years earlier. We had been there before for cookouts and various winter activities, but never to spend the night. We were excited—now we were going to have a chance to try our new skills at cooking, whittling, building fires, and pitching tents. In the back of both our minds, however, we knew we were facing an unknown test of courage, and once we crossed over that bridge, we could never go back.

Both Tom and I felt prepared for anything. We had taken our training seriously, and we had our multifunction tools at our sides. In addition, we had a plan to help each other if the situation called for it. We were confident that we could escape any nasty situations together.

The first campout in May was always well attended. Besides the adult leaders, the most senior scouts would be there. We were pretty sure it was their job to carry out the initiation, and we kept a close eye on them so we might discern any signs of impending trouble.

The evening of the first night was uneventful. We dined marvelously on venison burgers and baked potatoes that had been cooked in the coals. After the meal, we cleaned up, played some games, and hit the hay. We slept in a small pup tent with no floor that Tom and I had pitched together, using our various multifunction tools to help us along the way. We had cut pine boughs to make a mattress that would get us off the cold ground and they filled the tent with the sweet smell of pine needles and sap. Although we imagined something happening that night, it didn't seem as if anything was in the air. Just to be safe, I set up a couple of trip lines outside the tent with fishing line and attached the ends to the guy strings of the tent. I knew those would shake us awake in the night if we needed it. Friday night came and went without event, and I pulled the trip lines first thing in the morning so they wouldn't be noticed.

All the next day the entire troop played games, built rope bridges, went on a long scavenger hunt, and prepared a council fire for the evening's festivities. Then we cleaned up and placed our tinfoil dinners under the main fire to cook. After dinner and some camp songs, at last the storytelling began. We sat listening, as each story seemed scarier than the next.

Finally the last story of the evening began, and it was the scariest of all! In fact, it had to be told in whispers, and that's when we realized the initiation had begun. That's when the older scouts told us "The True Story of the Great Chief Aubbeenaubbee."

Southeast of Mogsinkeekeh
He began to take his wives,
At least one in every village,
Some say that there were five.
Soon he was a leader,
A man both brave and fair,
With long black braids
And feathers of the hawk,
Tied into his hair.

Some say he fought at Tippecanoe
With Nawtuck at his side,
Against Harrison at Old Fort Wayne,
He hoped to turn the tide.

But Harrison was mighty
With his thousand well-armed men,
And he broke the hope of the Indian,
Again and again and again.

Back home he took to drinking
And signing away his lands,
It was clear to him the white man
Had gained an upper hand,
His cage kept getting smaller
With nowhere else to go,
And one night he just went crazy,
Killed a wife with just one blow.

Old Aubbeenaubbee had been a fierce Potawatomi warrior in his prime, but, toward the end of his days, had turned to drink and went crazy, killing one of his wives in an argument.

Other chiefs were called together,
And sentenced him to death,
To be carried out by one of his sons,
Within the year or less.

As was Potawatomi custom, one of Aubbeenaubbee's kin was called upon to carry out the sentence. Under Native American law, however, the chief would have his life spared if he just went away and was never heard from again.

Old Aubbee took to hiding,
But he could not stay away,
When his daughter, Trisbee Rose,
Was to have her wedding day.

Unfortunately Aubbeenaubbee was drawn back home to see his daughter at her wedding. His son, Pawkooshuck, who was ordered to carry out the death sentence, was there.

At the feast, he soon grew wary,
Snuck away without a sound,
The moon had not yet risen,
The sun was going down,
Pawkooshuck followed after him,
With tomahawk in hand,
And at the Blodget tavern,
Brought down a broken man.

This was the really chilling part. His own son had followed him and waited until nightfall when Aubbeenaubbee was too hungover to wake up and sense danger. Then sneaking up behind him, Pawkooshuck raised his tomahawk and brought it down in the middle of his father's skull, crushing it.

The older scouts took turns telling the story with relish, their eyes wide as they spoke in hushed voices. They made sure we could see the hatchet come down on Old Aubbee's head, the blood spurting across the old cabin in every direction. After they had embellished the moment with great graphic detail, they continued.

They took Old Aubbeenaubbee
And set him against a tree,
Seventy-five years had come and gone,
His spirit wasn't free.
And on that cold October night,
When there's no moon out at all,
If you listen very closely,
You still can hear him call . . .

"It wasn't enough," they told us that night, "that old Aubbee was dead, because now his spirit is trapped and unable to leave this world. So now old Aubbee roams around at night, looking for others he can kill, so they can join him on his nightly marches around the area." At last, the moment of truth arrived, and they turned to all the new scouts, narrowed their eyes, and said:

"If you want to be a scout in Troop 257, you have to prove that you're brave enough to stand up to old Aubbee's ghost. We've planned a little night hike for you, and you won't be allowed to use flashlights."

The night hike they had in mind for our small group of inductees was no ordinary one; we were told we were to walk along the old railroad bed to Menominee's statue, about a half mile from the camp. We had to make the journey on our own and report back as soon as we returned.

Although there were six of us, none of us wanted to go. We all protested loudly, but it was no use.

We found the old track and crept along in the moonlight. Occasionally, the whole group would stop instinctively and listen to the night. Any small sound seemed amplified and dangerous. Once we heard an owl in the moonlight, another time we heard small rustlings in the woods.

As we neared the monument we prepared for the worst. All the way there Tom and I had our hands on our knives. We thought sure they would be waiting for us there. But nothing happened. It became apparent the ambush was planned for our return trip down the railroad bed.

When we got to the statue, I was secretly glad we had gone. The white granite statue of Menominee seemed noble and majestic in the moonlight rather than scary. In fact just staring at the statue made me feel courageous, and it was then that I figured out a way we could outsmart our party of ambushers.

"It's simple," I explained. "We just need to take the road back to camp. If we stay quiet, they won't figure it out, and we're sure to spoil their fun."

Hearing the plan, the rest of the scouts obliged and we took off walking silently and double-time, knowing that the road to camp was almost twice as long. When we arrived back at camp, it was clear our plan had worked; only the adult leaders sat around the council fire talking. When they saw us, one of the men excused himself and walked off toward the railroad tracks. When we asked about everyone else, the adults told us the others had gone on a stargazing hike. We knew they were lying, that we had outfoxed them, and come up clear winners. We all decided to turn in for the night and headed off to bed, well aware we had still best be on our guard.

When Tom and I got into the tent, he immediately began to talk.

"What do you think they'll do, man? Did you see their faces when we walked into camp? We got those guys royal!"

"But now they're going to be out for blood!" I grimaced.

"So . . . what should we do? We can't stay up all night?"

"No," I said, thinking fast, "but we can be prepared! Listen, I'm going to set up those trip wires again. You hold out the flashlight with me and let's look around." The camp seemed quiet. I slipped out and ran the fishing line around the pup tent, again fastening it to the guy wires of the tent. Then I ducked back inside.

"Now listen," I said, in a low voice. "You've got your flashlight and I've got my knife. If we hear them around the tent, let's just jump out, and let them know who's in charge!"

"Sounds like a plan," Tom agreed. "But what if we fall asleep?"

"Don't worry, we won't; besides, those guys aren't going to stay up all night," I reasoned. "Look, what we need to do is practice. I'll count to three, then you turn on your light and I'll pull my knife blade out."

"OK," Tom said, "let's try it."

"One, two, three . . ."

Tom pulled up his light and switched in on. I pulled out my knife.

"We nailed it," I said. "Let's try it again."

"One, two, three. . ."

Immediately Tom's light went on and the stainless steel blade glinted in the artificial light.

"I think we're ready, don't you?" Tom whispered.

"Yeah, as long as we don't sleep too soundly," I warned.

Minutes went by, then more minutes.

"Tom, you still awake?"

"Yeah," he mumbled, drifting off, "but not much longer."

I yawned heavily. I knew I was fading too, and before long we were fast asleep.

The next thing I heard was a thud and a moan outside the tent, as if someone had fallen. Then I heard the sound of a knife cutting our tent's guy wires and a loud drum banging in the distance. Its sound was drawing closer. I could feel the tent sagging on top of us.

"Tom, Tom!" I whispered loudly, but he was moaning and struggling to wake up. "Tom!" I poked him in the side. Now there were two drums pounding.

"Huh, huh?" he muttered.

"Your light, your light!"

Tom switched on the light, but he put it accidentally into the blinking mode. The light began to flash as I searched along my side for my knife. Outside the drums were pounding even louder.

"I can't find my knife!" I said. "We gotta get outta here!"

Finally I rolled over and felt the cold knife at my side; I grabbed it and shouted, "Come on, are you ready? Get that thing working!"

Now the drums sounded as if they were on top of us, getting louder and louder. Tom flicked the light switch the other direction and slithered toward the fallen doorway with me. We wriggled, like worms, batting at the heavy canvas and lifting the fallen tent pole in our way. We both slid out and into the night and quickly jumped to our feet, ready for whatever was coming. The drums pounded mercilessly. All around us stood scouts in war paint, holding fiery torches and chanting.

"UGG CHING-A-OO, AUBBEENAUBBEE, UGG CHING-A-OO AUBBEENAUBBEE!"

Suddenly, from out of the darkness, two painted figures ran toward us and immediately, before we could even react, drenched us with two large buckets of cold, cold water.

We stood there, stunned, in our T-shirts and white underwear, dripping from head to foot. Tom's failing light illuminated the faces of the other scouts who were laughing heartily at our predicament. I looked down at my multifunction knife. There, in the dim light I saw that I had pulled out . . . my spoon.

Oh Aubbeenaubbee,
"One Who Looks Behind,"
You've seen the truth
In the white man's eyes,
And it's eaten up your mind,
Oh Aubbeenaubbee,
Caught in-between,
The end of the Indian Nation,
And the beginning of the white man's dream.

That night I learned three important truths:

One: Despite all the training under your belt and your best-laid plans, you can only be so prepared.

Two: You have to be willing to laugh at yourself in the midst of your own best intentions—especially if you're standing in the woods wearing only wet underwear.

Three: Even though you're armed with the best multifunction tool in the world, it can't save you from a band of determined Indians.

George Schricker

George Schricker, a Northwestern University interdepartmental studies graduate, has practiced his original and creative work for over thirty years. He has performed poetry in bookstores and coffeehouses in New York City and Washington, D.C., told stories at numerous storytelling festivals, and sung songs with symphony orchestras in Indiana and Illinois. His essay, "A Muffled Humming Like the Droning of the Bees," appears in Where We Live: Essays about Indiana, *published by Indiana University Press. His latest children's recording is entitled,* George's Brother. *George lives in Plymouth, Indiana, with his wife, Michele, and son, Ezra. For more information visit www.heartmindproductions.com or write to heartmind@hoosierlink.net.*

GRANDPA'S BARN
Jim May

A night wind rippled the dark water in the irrigation ditch. The warm air lapped across the wheat field, gaining strength and coaxing the green, slender stalks to bend and sway, a hillside samba to the rising moon.

A force by the time it reached the old barn, the wind strained against the posts and beams. A low drone rose over the roof and hung over the farmstead like a keening for something lost on the vast expanse of prairie.

Janie lay in bed listening to the empty barn that her late grandfather had built when she heard something on the porch beneath her window—the rhythm of a rocking chair and the soft tapping of a slipper. Janie knew the sound. Grandma Sarah sat up nights when the wind was howling.

****

Janie woke to the sun shining through the lace curtains of her bedroom window and the birds in full chorus. She jumped out of bed. No school! She had graduated from eighth grade. Summer! Janie ran down the stairs to the kitchen where her grandma stood at the stove making pancakes for her dad. Grandma Sarah looked tired.

Her dad sat at the table jabbing at little maple soaked wedges with his fork 'til he had speared a mouthful. Skinny, but a big eater nonetheless, he could eat a dozen of his mother's griddle cakes. He chewed fast and gulped his coffee. Though the bulk of his corn crop was in, the spring had been a wet one, and he had one low, wet piece of ground left to plant.

Her grandma fixed Janie a plate of pancakes, then sat down, heavy in her chair, a mug of coffee in her hand.

"Didn't sleep good last night, again. I guess I got to figure my age is against me."

"I heard the wind last night, too, Grandma."

"Yes, dear. That wind blew so my bed shook. Couldn't sleep. I sat on the porch for a while. The robins started in singing about 4:30 and I just came right in and got the pancake batter goin'. I figured your father would want to get an early start. I'm always ready to work in the morning once the birds sing. I like summer; the nights are short and you can look forward to the birds gettin' you started."

Janie couldn't worry too much about her grandma's sleepless nights that first morning of her summer vacation. She had other things on her mind. During the next three months there'd be time to ride her pony.

She had ridden Banner, her pinto pony, since she was a little girl. They had the run of the farm and would gallop through the fields, ride out sometimes late at night or before sunrise. "Just don't go too far and be careful," her dad would warn when she'd ask to go riding at all hours.

The neighbors got used to seeing Janie and Banner, running flat out through the sweet clover and alfalfa, leaving grasshoppers dazed in their wake, and the dewy, morning air a wild kaleidoscope of flushed cabbage butterflies and monarchs.

But, as the summer days passed, Janie began to feel awkward on her pony. Her legs hung long down his sides, practically dragging on the ground. The tallest girl in her class, Janie just felt too big. Her grandma told her not to worry about it. "You're just tall and big-boned like your mother's side of the family"—her grandma's words didn't help.

She'd ride in the hay field alongside the gravel road watching for cars. If she saw a car boiling up the dust in the distance, she'd jump off Banner and lead him until the car passed. Janie didn't want to be seen all gangly on her little pony. She longed for a tall, graceful horse. She imagined sitting on her new mount, her back straight and boots in the stirrups.

That summer of her thirteenth year, Janie looked for grace wherever she could find it. In the twilight when the day would ease up slow and hazy and the barnyard turned quiet, except for the hogs banging the galvanized metal feeders as they nosed for their supper, Janie would watch the barn swallows—streamlined little birds that slipped through the sweet manure air on deep blue, greasy wings, riding the heat that rose from the bodies of the steers and the warm, black dirt.

Sometimes, she'd daydream about flying, or racing thoroughbreds, or playing on the girls' basketball team. In the winter her best girlfriend's dad had taken her and her girlfriend to the high school gym to watch a girls' game. Janie had loved the gym the minute she stepped through the big steel doors and took in the wide varnished floor, the sounds of the pep band and cheering, and the smell of popcorn and bubble gum.

Janie sat in the bleachers, hardly able to speak, her eyes fixed on the varsity players. They moved fast, with a strength and casual sureness that Janie had sometimes felt when riding and had seen in some farm women who worked the fields and handled cattle and tractors.

Janie saw her father's MVP photo on the gym wall that night. Her dad had been the best basketball player at the high school and had played one year in college: he quit school to come back to the farm and get married.

Grandma Sarah had fretted about her son's new wife: "She's so young, and from town, besides." Janie's mother had run off after a year.

The day after the basketball game, Janie walked around the farm looking for a place to hang a basketball hoop. She knew she couldn't dribble on the dirt and gravel in the yard, and the dairy barn was filled with hay for the milk cows.

So Janie figured she'd ask her dad to put up a hoop in the old, empty barn, the one her grandpa and grandma had built when they "first went farmin'," as Grandma used to say. Her grandpa had used it for his draft horses and to store hay in the loft. Small and weathered gray, the barn still had the old wooden horse stalls below. It stood at the edge of the yard, between the house and the hay field, like an ancient monument, a buttress against the west wind.

Once, years before, Janie had peeked through a window of the barn. She remembered cobwebs hanging everywhere from the beams and rafters, loose hay in piles, and the wind, like a caroling of whispers seeping through long slats of light in the walls, stirring up dust and rot. She only looked for a moment before the sound of the wind scared her into running back to the house.

Her father had seen her and scolded her at the supper table, "You stay out of there. It's dangerous," he said. "Nothing but loose floor boards and rusty nails." She had not thought about the barn again—until she saw the girls' basketball team.

She imagined herself dribbling a ball on the smooth floorboards in the haymow. She figured that the bad planks could be replaced. Nailing a hoop and backboard to the side of a wall would be the easiest part.

Finally, one evening in late winter as the February wind carried soft air from the gulf, Janie brought the subject up at the supper table. After all, she had hardly thought of anything else since seeing that basketball game.

"It's almost as big as a gym up in the haymow and there's hardly any hay." She became more excited as she talked out loud. "I'm saving up for a ball and hoop." Her father listened in silence, his head bowed, stirring his stewed tomatoes with his spoon. Janie heard her grandma's fork rattling against her plate and looked across the table. Her grandma's hands trembled, faced flushed.

"There's plenty of work around here for you to do," grandma said. "You don't have time for boys' games. I don't want any accidents in that barn."

Janie and her grandma had always been close. As a toddler she had shadowed the old woman in the house dress, followed her around from room to room and out in the yard, never more than a few feet behind. "That's my helper, right there," Grandma would say when neighbors came to visit or to buy eggs—"I got the boss with me today." Now Grandma sat at the table, her eyes unfocused, staring at the blank wall.

That night at the supper table, Janie felt ashamed for asking about the barn, and she didn't bring the subject up again. She tried to forget about basketball. When summer came, she rode her pony every day. "I don't know what we're going to do, Banner. You're done growin' and I'm not." Still, she loved riding on those first sweet, warm summer days.

It was on one of those summer days that she saw dust boiling up in the distance as she trotted Banner along the gravel road that ran in front of their farm.

She hopped off her pony. Leading him by the reins, she watched the car approach, a distant speck chased by a ball of billowing dust that grew into a long, languid tail that floated above the roadway before settling on the dark-green corn rows. Finally, she saw that it was not a car at all but an old, chalky-blue Chevrolet pickup. Janie knew that truck belonged to Jockey, the horse trader.

Janie always looked forward to his visits. She'd listen in when Jockey "chewed the fat," as he called it, with her dad after supper or in the morning after chores. Jockey talked of horse trades and his travels. He never missed an auction in that county. Once, when Janie was a little girl, he brought her a corncob doll. He usually had a brown bag full of candy corn in the cab of his truck—big yellow, orange, and white kernels that Janie only got at Halloween and when Jockey came over.

Janie waved and the pickup slowed as it pulled alongside her. Jockey brought the truck to a stop, rolled the window down, and said, "You know, a little horse that you've got to pull along behind you is worse than having no horse a'tall."

Janie laughed, "Well, Jockey, if you'd do your horse trading business with my dad, you'd trade him a horse my size so I wouldn't have to drag this pony around."

"Now you may have something there. I haven't been moving much livestock lately. Maybe that's what they mean when they say that horse trading is a healthy way to make a living because you almost always outlive your money." Jockey's face puckered and his shoulders hunched a bit as he chuckled at his own joke.

"I gotta go now, Janie. Gotta see a fella over at the county seat about a load of heifers that I bought. I'll stop by your place tomorrow to take a look at that scrap-iron pile of yours. I'm going to take a load of iron into the city on Friday."

Jockey rolled his window back up and the truck bumped and rattled down the dirt road, finally making enough dust to disappear.

Janie jumped on Banner and galloped back to the house.

The next day, sure to his word, Jockey's pickup rolled into the yard. He gave Janie a "Howdy" through the open window, brought the truck to a rolling stop, and stepped out.

He moved slowly. He was short and wiry like a real jockey, but the years and cheeseburgers he loved had given him a round little belly perched about in the middle of his gray-striped bib overalls. His head was completely bald except for a thick band of white hair that grew around the bottom of his railroad hat—one of those men who seemed to have two completely different faces depending upon whether he wore his hat or not.

Jockey followed Janie to her scrap-iron pile, a cluttered, untidy stack of rusty, greasy odds and ends, mostly from broken-down farm machinery.

"Well, that's a nice heap," he said, "and the price of scrap is up about three pennies this week. I'd say it'd be worth about twenty-five dollars just as she sits."

"Twenty-five," Janie hollered in mock horror. "I think you'd practically be stealing it for two hundred."

"Twenty-five and a half, take it or leave it!"

"Sold!" Janie laughed and the two of them shook hands.

Janie knew the money would be enough to buy a basketball, so she told Jockey about wanting to try out for the girls' team in the fall.

"Now that's a good idea, Janie. Why I knew a little girl over at the high school who was quite a player. She even got a scholarship to college and she wasn't as tall as you. Ya got to practice, though. Practice every day; that's the way to do it. Shoot the ball at the hoop everyday, over and over again. Ya got to get a shot, Janie. Ya got to get a shot."

"Jockey, I didn't know you played!"

"Well, I didn't but that don't keep me from knowin' all about it," Jockey grinned, his eyes twinkling. "Truth is I wasn't in school long, but I was on the church team when I was a kid and I'm still pretty quick." He gave a little step forward and then rocked back, his arm raised, his hands holding an invisible basketball; he looked over at Janie and gave her a wink.

"I was a guard, a ball handler."

Since he seemed all for the idea, Janie confided that she had no place to hang a basketball hoop or to practice dribbling. Jockey took in Janie's problem for a moment and then his face brightened. "The old horse barn there would work." He pointed to the gray building.

Janie told him how she had asked her father if she could use the barn, but he seemed against it. She told her old friend how her grandma had acted that night at the supper table when Janie had asked about putting a hoop in the barn.

"I don't want Grandma to worry."

Jockey didn't reply at first, his face frozen in an expression that revealed nothing of his thoughts or feelings. He looked past Janie like he was fixing his eyes on some distant point over her shoulder. They were both quiet. Then Jockey dropped his chin and smiled. He reached into his pocket and took out his jackknife. He wiped off the blade on his overalls as he studied the ground around his feet. Spotting a corncob, he went for it, slowly bending at the waist, letting out a breathy grunt as he squatted to pick it up. He whittled the end of the cob with careful concentration, as if the act of working the little blade was organizing his thoughts and intentions.

"Well, that old barn could be used all right, should be used!" His voice grew stern. "It's a shame to let it just stand empty, no cattle or nothin'. A barn or a house needs to have life in it or it'll go bad." He coughed and hung his head and shoulders like something was weighing him down, his arms and hands limp on each side so that he almost dropped the corncob and knife. Then he went back to whittling, carefully watching each little cut of his jackknife.

"It's nobody's fault what happened in that barn, Janie, just one of those things. Whaddya gonna do about somethin' like that?"

Janie felt a knot rise in her stomach and creep up toward her throat.

Jockey looked up from his knife and corncob and caught Janie's eyes. He sighed; "Lord, she don't know," was the unwelcome thought.

"Ah, I guess it's all between you and your dad and grandma, Janie. I suppose I should just stay out of it."

"Why, Jockey? What happened in the barn? They never talk about things."

Jockey looked back up at this skinny, awkward farm girl with the slightly stooped shoulders. She looked scared, standing there in an old flannel shirt with a torn pocket. Her eyes were intent and pleading.

She had always been his favorite of the young ones that he liked to tease on his farm business visits. She had a certain stubborn grittiness, along with the generosity that he had known in her grandparents.

"Your grandpa was a good man, Janie; that was before your time. Has your dad or grandma talked about him?"

"No. They just seem to miss him, I guess. Can't talk much. My father is pretty quiet. Grandma too."

"He was a worker. People hardly knew nothin' but work in those days. But your grandparents were doin' good: They was startin' a family.

"I watched the old barn go up, and after that the fruit trees along the side yard and flowers and lilac bushes around the porch. Your grandma always had a way of growing somethin'. The two of them would be sittin' on the porch in the evening and see me ride by on my bicycle. They'd wave me over every time and make me sit with them. Your grandma always had lemonade and an apple or cookie for me.

"Then the Depression came." Jockey studied the blade of his pocketknife.

"Everybody got hit; the farmers had food to eat, which was better off than some, but the prices they was gettin' for crops and milk went down to nothin', and then the drought. Farmers'd borrow from the bank just to pay for the seed and fertilizer; then they'd watch the corn and hay burn up in the field, white as ash. The banks went down too.

"They say your grandpa got so he couldn't stand to come into the house 'cause your grandma would be sittin' over the bills, figuring with her pencil, and crying into her apron. So he'd stay late in the barn talkin' to the horses.

"A lot of farmers lost hope back then—nothin' to be ashamed of. Sometimes a man gets pushed right to the edge. Sometimes there are moments, days, or weeks scattered through a life when you lose hope. You got to get through those days any way you can, Janie. Things will usually get better eventually if you just see it through. Most of life is just keepin' goin'.

"Nobody had money. Your grandpa'd have some of us younger boys from town come and do a little work at the farm. Ya see, he knew that our families couldn't feed us because they had to feed the younger ones. He'd have us chop wood or cut thistles, something to keep us busy 'til the middle of the day—dinnertime.

Then when your grandma'd ring the bell, he'd say, 'Let's go eat boys. That's why we work, so we can eat.'

"Your gram would put on quite a spread. We'd have warm biscuits and dinner rolls, all kinds of fresh garden greens or put-up vegetables in the winter, new potatoes with bacon grease and ham hocks, apple pie, canned peaches; it was something to see. And we ate like starving dogs. Sometimes it was the only meal we'd have in a day or two."

Jockey had whittled the corncob down to a nub. He threw it away, folded his knife and put it back in his pocket.

"I seen it start with your grandpa after the drought. He'd just get quiet all of a sudden. He was a great whistler, loved to whistle tunes when we were out working, any tune you could imagine—stuff he learned off the radio. Halloween would come and he could whistle up sounds like ghosts and the wind blowing through the graveyard to make your grandma shiver and giggle.

"When it got so dry and the crops burned, he stopped whistling. He'd sit quiet on the porch in the heat for hours—his rocking chair making tracks in the dust.

"He wanted something to leave your dad. He used to say, 'It's a heck of a thing to have nothin' to leave your kids.' He always said he wanted to leave your dad this land—somethin' that'd been sweated over."

Jockey brushed some gravel into a pile with one foot and then patted the stones down with the other.

"He was like a father to me." Jockey turned away and wiped his nose with his shirtsleeve. "I wished he would have called me that day. He hanged himself there in the barn. That's why your folks leave it be. He was a good man, Janie."

Janie's chin dropped to her chest. Her ears rang and the tight feeling at the bottom of her throat became a heavy lump forcing her to swallow. She wanted to run, but her feet seemed planted right there in the dirt of the barnyard. Head down, she listened as Jockey told her more.

"He could have made it, I think, if he'd asked for help. His brothers came out from town and kept the farm goin', the payments up. They made a livin' at it after the war; tractors were cheap and they built a new dairy barn. Then your dad took it over.

"I don't think your grandpa ever asked for their help right at the end. His brothers were strugglin', too. He didn't want to put them out, I suppose. He always was thinkin' of the other guy. Didn't want to get in anybody's way."

Janie felt dizzy and heartsick for her grandpa and Grandma Sarah. She suddenly longed for her mother. Hot tears flooded her eyes and ran down her cheeks. She could hear herself sobbing as she turned and ran to the house, calling out a choked, "Bye Jockey," over her shoulder.

Jockey stood there by the shed for a long time—a small, old man with white hair, his arm braced against the little asphalt-sided building. Finally, he loaded the scrap iron onto the pickup, single piece by single piece with the slow delicacy and precision of an aged laborer. He left a twenty dollar bill, a five, and a fifty-cent piece in the mailbox.

Janie had trouble sleeping that night. She hadn't said a thing at the supper table. "I saw you and Jockey visitin'. What were ya talkin' about?" her grandma asked.

Janie blurted, "About basketball," then excused herself from the table, and ran upstairs to her room.

Jockey hadn't slept well either.

That next day he drove his stock truck over to Janie's place. Though hesitant to come out of the house, she couldn't resist finding out what Jockey had in the big, double-axle truck with the wooden livestock rack.

While Janie stood watching, Jockey climbed out of the cab and walked around to the back of the truck. He took the pins out of the long tailgate and lowered it onto the ground. Janie could hear a horse stomping and snorting as she watched Jockey climb up into the truck. She caught her breath when the old trader appeared at the back of the box leading a yellow horse with a black mane and tail and a delicate, dished head.

"She's a two-year-old, Janie, a filly comin' to be a mare just like you. She's going to be tall and fast."

The young animal slowly picked her way down the steep, wooden planks, head down, snorting and trembling, big wide-set, brown eyes alert and steady. The buckskin hesitated at the bottom of the ramp near the ground, raised her forelegs into the air, pushed off with her hind legs and landed softly on the solid ground where she immediately gathered herself, and, after a good shake of her coat, perked her ears forward to investigate the new surroundings. Jockey made some clicking noises to her and led the horse in a big circle around Janie. He handed Janie the lead strap, then he walked around the horse, patting her neck, flanks, and rump, talking to her all the time.

"Now you hang on to her while I go talk to your father."

That day Jockey made Janie's dad a real good deal, and Janie had her horse—a buckskin beauty.

For the next few weeks of the summer Janie didn't think much about the barn or basketball but spent all of her spare time grooming the filly, leading her about the place, and treating her to carrots.

****

One night in early August, Janie lay on her bed with the window open. The week had brought hot, cicada-buzzing weather—the birds nearly silent except for the occasional plaintive call of a wood peewee from the trees behind the barn.

All afternoon Janie had watched towering thunderheads build to the west. She heard distant rumblings and looked forward to the cool, clean air that would come with the storm. At about nine o'clock a squall line approached, rolling across the hay field. Janie could hear the rain hitting the corn a mile away and then bone-rattling thunder shook the house.

The smell of cool, green air filled the room. Then the wind shifted and the rain came in force, slanting through the window, soaking the sill, dresser, and bed. When Janie hurried across the room to slam down the sash, she saw her filly running loose down in the yard—neck arched, tail raised, prancing and wavy through the window pane.

Janie jumped into her jeans, bounded down the stairs and ran out the kitchen door.

The filly bolted when it first saw Janie but eventually stood still enough for Janie to grab its halter. She gave the frisky animal a mild scolding for escaping the barn and led the horse back into the stall where she closed the top and bottom half doors to keep out the rain. She patted down the wet, trembling filly with handfuls of straw, all the while calming her with a low, easy voice.

After awhile, the loud drumming on the barn roof slowed to a sporadic tapping. Horse and girl stayed put—two yearlings waiting out the storm.

When it seemed quiet again, Janie opened the top half door and let out a little wide-eyed gasp that made the horse's head rise up and its ears stand. The storm had cleared the air of everything between heaven and earth and the black, clear sky had filled with stars. Janie leaned over the half door to see more.

The filly stuck her head out the opening, too. Janie moved toward her horse so its whiskers and breathing tickled her cheek. The animal and the girl took in the clean, flowery air, and the star-sprinkled dome of the sky. The filly's soft nose nudged Janie's hair. At that moment she felt like the luckiest girl in the world.

Then the kitchen light went on, casting a soft, orange net that dissolved the darkness. Janie and the young, curious horse watched Grandma Sarah walk across the kitchen to the screen door. Then Janie heard it—the wind, strong again on the tail of the storm, howling across the roof of grandpa's barn.

Janie watched her grandma walk onto the porch and then down the steps, heading right toward the old barn. Her back straight and her gait steady as she crossed the yard and then up the earthen ramp to the large barn doors that opened to the haymow. Her grandma pushed hard on one of them; it seemed stuck on its rusty track, frozen. Grandma Sarah pushed again and then, spreading her feet for leverage, leaned hard against the door. Though troubled by what she saw, Janie smiled at her grandmother's strength as one of the doors moved enough to form a dark, empty column that seemed to swallow the old woman.

Janie opened the stall door and quickly slipped out before the filly could follow. She latched the door and ran hard toward the old barn. The wind was gaining strength, and Janie ran against it. She retraced her grandmother's steps through the two doors. Inside the floor felt rough under her feet, and all around her was the sound of the wind and a stirring of hay chaff and dust.

A gauzy moonbeam powdered through a missing rib of the building, revealing a rope that dangled from a cross beam; its length twirling slowly in the silver dust. Under the rope, and a little to the side, her Grandma Sarah stood loosening a knot that bound the other end to a post. The knot, tied by weary hands doing their last work, had dried and stiffened through the years. When it finally released, the old woman began to pull, hand over hand. High across the beam the frayed end slowly shortened and then slipped back over the timber. The old hemp swooned and then fell limp onto the floorboards. Janie watched her grandmother gather the rope to her breast and then collapse.

Janie ran to her. She lay there so still that Janie gave her a rough shake. "Grandma! Grandma!"

Her grandma gave a start and then, still clutching the rope in one hand, she threw her other arm around her granddaughter's shoulder and held tight, burying her head into Janie's neck. Slow, liquid sobs turned to squeals that sounded like a little girl. She cried in Janie's arms for a long time.

After enough she began to speak. "I'm sorry, sweetheart."

"It's OK, Grandma. Everything's OK. Jockey told me."

Grandma sat up, looked at Janie a long moment, then took a hanky from her apron pocket and blew her nose.

"No. It ain't OK. You need a place to play your basketball, to have some fun in your life. We all worked too hard. 'Course we didn't mind back then. We thought we was makin' somethin' good. Somethin' that could last."

Grandma Sarah spoke of how she and her husband had built the barn, cutting the logs from the south woodlot and dragging them to the fieldstone foundation site with the old team, Buttermilk and Maude.

"He loved that team! He was like you, Janie, when it came to horses. Oh Janie, he would have been so proud of you!"

She brought her hanky back up to her eyes, lowered her head for a moment, and then spoke again about trimming the logs with ax and adz until they were squared off and ready for the day the neighbors would come. The day of the barn raising, men with ropes and crowbars, busy like Lilliputians, set the heavy timbers in place. Long tables under the shade trees displayed the pride of every kitchen. By sunset they had a barn to shelter the draft horses whose brute strength and companionship would act as a lever against the ominous task of making the land yield a living.

And how after the barn was up, she and Janie's young grandfather sat with their coffee on the front porch among the hollyhocks and basked in the fragrance of the new wood, admiring the sight of the miraculous barn where there had been only sky the day before.

"So, Jockey told you?"

"Yes, Grandma."

"I guess it's all for the best that you know—now that you've seen this sorry old rope."

*****

When Janie's father came down for breakfast the next morning, Grandma Sarah and Janie were waiting for him. Grandma built a small kindling fire in the kitchen woodstove and threw the rope into the firebox. The little family sat and watched the thick cord glow and burn.

They didn't see the smoke rise out of the chimney, drift over the misty, morning fields, over the corn flowers and hay stubble, over the creek, and over the black-and-white calf suckling its mother in the pasture.

That afternoon Janie's father swept away the loose hay from the mow in the old barn and replaced the weakened floorboards.

From late summer through the evenings of early autumn Grandma Sarah would sit in her rocker on the porch listening to Janie bounce the basketball and rattle the iron hoop in the old barn.

Sitting in her rocking chair on the porch, surrounded by her mums and asters, Grandma Sarah would reflect on how well that barn had held up over the years.

That was the summer that Janie learned to play basketball. It was the summer she learned that her grandfather had been a good man: She wished she had known him.

Epilogue

Out of the Rain
Jim May

I always liked the old barn
The empty, powdery cow yard
Boards missing, ribs combing the air
A sieve for the west wind as it passed through

Forgotten skeleton with hay from horse-drawn harvests
Hanging here and there like loose flesh

I thought I'd stay awhile out of the rain
Then I spied the milking stool on the stained floor
Tipped on its side like a baby's chair or an oaken dwarf seat

I thought of my dad sitting with his legs under the cow
His head and cap braced against the flanks of the Holstein,
Milking

The silky sandpaper sound of milk careening into the empty bucket

He spoke of the Depression

Of the men, the young men, the old men
The sons of fathers, the sons and grandsons of farmers
Who, losing the farm, had stood on milking stools
Made themselves hay twine nooses
And stepped off into the sweet empty space above the lime floor
Their work boots hanging in the sweet manure air
Their boots kicking, perhaps reaching for the stool
To milk again

But too late to change their mind. Their boots hang still
The son of a farmer, the father of sons
Stretched from the beam, almost to the floor

The president of the bank
He hanged himself, too

Jim May

Jim May lives in Harvard, Illinois, with his wife, visual artist Nan Seidler. The path of the full-time, professional storyteller has been his since 1985, and has taken him across the United States, and to Europe, Canada, and Mexico. May received a Chicago Emmy Award for the Chicago Public Television production of his original story: "A Bell for Shorty." His collection of family stories, Farm on Nippersink Creek *(August House, 1994) received a Best Book award from the Public Library Association. For more information visit www.storytelling.org/jimmay or contact him at maystory@earthlink.net.*

THE PIPELINE BLUES: A MIDWEST STORY OF ENVIRONMENTAL TRIUMPH

Beth Horner

This is the story of a small town
Like so many towns all around
That grew 'til it was burstin' at the seams.
This is the story of my hometown
That went one way, then turned around
And said, "Show me a better way to be."
And this is a story about a song
Written, sung, came along
And totally changed the scene.
"O, Columbia, the Gem of the Ocean."

I was born in the town of Columbia, Missouri. It is nowhere near the ocean. It's smack-dab in the middle of Boone County, which is smack-dab in the middle of the state of Missouri, which is smack-dab in the middle of the United States. Throughout its history Missouri has been an agricultural state. However, much of the rocky, hilly land is not particularly conducive to farming. As a result Missouri has never been an overly prosperous state. Those rocks and hills are beautiful though, and the rivers and streams that run in and out of them are even prettier.

When my parents first moved to Boone County in 1946, Columbia had a population of approximately 20,000. For them the most exciting day of the week was Saturday, Market Day, when everyone would come to town and spend all day selling, buying, trading, visiting, and catching up on the news at the county courthouse square. At that time Columbia boasted two hotels, two restaurants serving evening meals, and no bars (liquor by the drink being illegal). If you were planning to have a baby, you had your choice of one and only one doctor, Jim Baker. I was delivered by our friend Doctor Baker in 1953, in the single, unair-conditioned delivery room of the tiny county hospital on the edge of town. Since it was ninety-nine degrees the day I was born, the experience created a lasting memory for my mother.

In addition to farming, Columbia's other "industry" was the University of Missouri and its world-famous journalism school. Over the years, the university added a law school, medical school, nursing school, and other educational opportunities, bringing people into town. By the time I graduated from Columbia's only public high school (Hickman High School, home of the fighting Kewpie Dolls) in 1971, the town's population had tripled to nearly 60,000. Columbia remained small town in its orientation though.

I left Boone County shortly afterward to make my way in the world, but I returned in the mid-1980s and was stunned to find that the "little" town of Columbia had become a busy, bustling, vital city with almost 90,000 people! I barely recognized the rocky hills that had once been dotted with rather unprosperous family farms and were now blanketed with hotels, motels, industries, housing subdivisions, shopping malls, cuisine from Texan to Taiwanese, enough bars to earn it the title "party town of central Missouri," and three large hospital complexes with hundreds of doctors and all types of alternative medicine as well.

The by-products of all this expansion in population, industry, and housing were low unemployment, prosperity, cultural opportunities, AND . . . sewage.

Ah . . . sewage. You know, on the average day, we average Joes and Janes do not really think all that much about sewage. It is just one of those things that exists on the periphery of our thoughts. We are aware that it happens and we hope that someone is taking care of it. It is simply not in the realm of our everyday thinking—unless it happens to show up in the realm of our own backyard . . . or our favorite fishing creek.

In 1987 a fellow went out to fish in his favorite fishing creek, Perche Creek, one of Boone County's pretty little creeks. He was about to drop his fishing pole into the creek when he stopped dead still. As far as he could see, all the way upstream and all the way downstream, Perche Creek was filled with dead fish, hundreds of dead fish!

The State Department of Natural Resources was called onto the scene, and soon it came to light that the city of Columbia was dumping partially treated sewage into Perche Creek. A little history: just five years previous to this incident, the city management had realized that Columbia's sewage treatment plant was unable to keep up with the city's industry and population growth. So the city hired the out-of-town engineering firm of Black and Veatch to design and build a brand-new, state-of-the-art, all-the-bells-and-whistles, never-go-out-of-date, multimillion-dollar sewage treatment plant. Five years later the sewage situation was already beyond the new plant's capacity. So the city started dumping partially treated sewage into Perche Creek, which then flowed into the Missouri River.

State officials declared a 3,211 fish kill in the seven-mile stretch of Perche Creek between Columbia's "new" treatment plant and the Missouri River, stated that the volume of sewage the city was dumping into the creek was legally too much for the volume of water in the creek, fined the city $17,000, and said "You've got to come up with a different answer to your sewage problem and it's got to be legal." So what is a city manager to do? He went back out of town to the firm of Black and Veatch and said, "Hey, we've got to come up with a different plan." The Black and Veatch team researched the situation, looked at the city's budget, looked at the law, and came up with a solution.

The grand solution: the city of Columbia would build a pipeline—six feet in diameter, six miles long—and pipe its partially treated sewage directly into the Missouri River, thus bypassing Perche Creek and the city's legal problem. "Not only is this legal," explained the Black and Veatch team, "but you can get federal funding for it under the Clean Water Act." However, the chance to get this funding was about to run out. The city manager realized that he had to get the city council to vote on the plan, apply for the money, and make it a done deal or they were going to lose the opportunity for federal money.

In fact it just about was a done deal until one night at a city council meeting, late in the evening, after all of the council's official business had been conducted, a quiet, unassuming man with a beard and wire-rimmed glasses stood up. "I live," he said, "in the town of Lupus, Missouri (lupus being Latin for wolf), right on the Missouri River. The Missouri River is so pretty in Lupus that people come from all over the state to fish, swim, and boat. In fact there is a state-owned recreational island just off of Lupus. Lupus has been my home for ten years."

"I've been doing a little research. And according to my research, if Columbia builds this pipeline, it is going to be dumping into the river each day, about two and a half miles upstream from Lupus, 13½ million gallons of half-treated sewage. Now I know they say that the solution to pollution is dilution, but I don't think two and a half miles—about thirty minutes river time—is going to do it.

"I've been doing a little research about what's going to go into that half-treated sewage. Of course there's going to be the chlordane that runs off from the foundations of houses, used for termite treatment, and also the runoff from agricultural pesticides and herbicides. Then, a big part of it is going to be the industrial waste water from the new industry and housing subdivisions in Columbia not to mention what flows down the drains of the three hospital complexes in town.

"So, according to my research, if Columbia builds this pipeline, it's going to be dumping into the river each day, thirty minutes upstream from Lupus, 13½ million gallons of chlordane, chromium, cadmium, copper, lead, mercury, nickel, zinc, cyanide, arsenic, . . . and human waste."

"Who is this guy?" one city council member whispered to another. The man went on. "Now if you study your geography, you'll notice that further on downstream is our state capital, Jefferson City. I'm sure that you know, of course, that Jefferson City pulls its drinking water right out of the river. And I guess you know that the aquifer beds for Columbia's own drinking water are just below the point at which that pipeline will be dumping into the river." He looked up from his notes into the faces of the city council members. They stared back at him.

"Who is this guy? Do you know this guy?" they asked themselves. The city council members looked carefully at "this guy." The question, "Who is this guy?" was a good one. Who was that guy? Looking at him, council members had a sneaking suspicion that this was a person who lived some sort of progressive, alternative lifestyle. And they feared that underneath that suit and vest there lurked a tie-dyed T-shirt . . . and not one that had been purchased recently. In other words, he looked like an old hippie.

Because . . . he was an old hippie. His name was Doug Elley. What they did not know about him was that he was also an environmental specialist for the Air Pollution Control Program at the State Department of Natural Resources, mayor of Lupus (thus representing his entire constituency of forty-nine people), and well known in some circles around the country as the inventor of the famous "sky crapper," a solar-assisted composting toilet. So, he was indeed familiar with the subject of sewage. However, whether it was because they did not like the way he looked, did not know anything about him, or did not understand what he was saying, they did not pay much attention to him.

At the next meeting, "that guy" was back. "I've been doing a little research," he said, "about sewage treatment. I found out about this fellow out in Woods Hole, Massachusetts, who's been experimenting with a marshlands/wetlands kind of sewage treatment—where you take cattails, freshwater shrimp, water hyacinth, snails, and certain kinds of fish and you flood the sewage into the marshland. Mother Nature then goes to work on it, plants and creatures eating up the toxic chemicals and human waste, so that what comes out the other side is clean water."

"Oh no. That guy is back," the city council members whispered to each other. "Why is he back, what is he talking about and who put him on the agenda?"

It just so happened that on that night, there was a young newspaper reporter named Tracy Barnett covering the meeting. The next morning, a small notice regarding Elley's idea for a wetland sewage treatment system appeared in the *Columbia Daily Tribune*.

At the next city council meeting, not only was "that guy" back, but he also brought another guy along with him: Hank Ottinger, president of the Columbia Sierra Club, university professor, environmental activist, and dynamic speaker. As Elley would later say, "Hank and I met when I presented the wetlands idea to the Sierra Club. From that night on, we formed a perfect fit of passion and professorial persuasion."

These "guys" simply would not go away. They returned to the city council meetings, meeting after meeting after meeting, expounding on the advantages of a wetlands sewage treatment system. And that newspaper reporter, Barnett, kept writing up the information they were expounding. In the weeks that followed, her articles grew from little notices to half paragraphs to full paragraphs to headline feature articles about sewage treatment. But who reads that stuff? If you see "sewage" in a headline, do your eyes gravitate directly to that article? Not likely. Hardly anyone paid her articles any attention.

Elley and Ottinger kept returning to city council meetings until one night the Black and Veatch folks explained that a wetlands sewage treatment plan would not work for two reasons. Number one, it had never been tried anywhere in this country in a town the size of Columbia. Number two, the Clean Water Act would not provide funding to build a wetlands sewage treatment system. The act would only provide funding to bypass Perche Creek with a pipeline and dump the city's partially treated sewage directly into the Missouri River. Council members noted, "We've got to move ahead and vote on this or we are going to lose our opportunity to apply for federal funding!"

So what is a city council member to do? City councils are made up of average Joes and Janes like you and me. For example, the mayor at the time ran a tree-trimming business. Who is one to believe—some "alternative-looking" guy from Lupus? Or the sewage experts? So that was the night that the Columbia City Council voted six to one to build a pipeline and dump its partially treated sewage directly into the Missouri River.

This vote irritated Elley. This vote irritated Ottinger. This vote irritated Barnett. And smack-dab in the middle of Columbia, in a house on Richardson

Lane, behind a newspaper, that irritation reached a songwriter.

If I could give any little bit of advice in life, it would be this: don't ever irritate a songwriter. This particular songwriter's name was Jerome Wheeler. Wheeler was well known around Columbia for his unique songwriting ability, his distinctive Boone County accent and the fact that he'd had an actual Top 40 hit in the 1960s. He had once formed a band named Cesspool Baker and later, another band called The River Cowboys. So, one could say that Wheeler has a natural interest in the subject of sewage and rivers. In fact he was one of the very few people in town who was actually reading Barnett's newspaper articles and following the sewage controversy. When Wheeler read that the city council had voted six to one to build the pipeline, he got irritated.

So he got out of his comfy chair, strung a clothesline across his living room, pinned up all of Barnett's newspaper articles that he had been saving, booted up his little Apple II GS computer, rang up Elley to get some pertinent information, picked up his guitar, and began to write a song. Over the next week and a half, and after attending a city council meeting to familiarize himself with the "characters in this scenario," Wheeler finished his song. Late one night, he delivered a cassette to Columbia's listener-supported radio station, KOPN. The next morning, people all over Columbia woke up to Wheeler's very unique voice singing his new song.

Talkin' Columbia City Pipeline Blues

Well, I ran into a thirsty man,
All hot and sweaty, said, "Mister, can
You tell me if there's a water fountain near?"
I said, "I don't mean to raise a stink
But I'd pass on havin' some water to drink.
You'd be better off drinking any other place but here."

Well, I could tell by the stupefied look in his eye,
He wasn't gonna let that one pass him by.
He said, "Really," he said, "What's to fear?"
I said, "The Pipeline Blues with a capital P
By the gem of the ocean with a capital C."
He said, "Tell me about it. This I gotta hear."

I said, "Columbia's got a sewer to the ocean
Full of dooo doo doo dooo doo doo doo."

Well, Doug Elley testified
'Bout the quality of life on the riverside
Being affected by all those effluents floatin' downstream.
You remember as kids we had to clear the pool,
Well, be thinkin' of that when you flush your stool.
You'll get a good idea of what I mean.

But the DNR and EPA
just want it all to go away.
Somebody ought to tell the governor he's livin' downstream.
I mean, we got babies to wash and dishes and such
But the city manager said we're askin' too much
Besides, he says, "What's wrong with water that's . . . sorta clean?"

So Columbia's got a sewer to the ocean
Full of dooo doo doo dooo doo doo doo.

I say, "Pack up your pipeline, your chemicals too.
Go back to doin' what Mother Nature used to do
With nothing more than gravity and time."
(A wetland!)
Anything but this pipeline scheme,
Dumpin' all the sewage in the muddy river stream.
The folks downstream think it's a crime.

But the city council said their hands are tied.
Black and Veatch are the ones to decide.
And the mayor looked like he'd be happier up a tree.
So there they went, votin' six to one
To go for those available federal funds
They might lose if they wait, research and see.

Columbia's got a sewer to the ocean
Full of dooo doo doo dooo doo doo doo.

Well, Mister Black and Mister Veatch
Stand to make more money each
Than most folks make 'round here in a year.
They can't recommend nothin' new, I guess
'Cause they're getting more and we're getting less,
And they don't even live around here.

So the next time you flush your stool,
Be thinkin' about us Boone County fools,
Who have to drink downstream from our latrine.
Well, one of these days, it's gonna be too late
To clean up the river with the name of the state.
No amount of money is ever gonna get it clean.

So pick up your bags, pack up your cans.
Go off to the woods, sit on your hands.
Bide your time 'till saner minds prevail.
We coulda had us a model plan
That benefited our fellow man,
But Columbia, we looked our trouble right in the eye . . . and we failed.

Columbia's got a sewer to the ocean
Full of dooo doo doo dooo doo doo doo.

Well, that would be a very clear image to wake up to first thing in the morning . . . as you are combing your hair, brushing your teeth, and sipping your coffee. It is catchy though! If you heard that two or three times, you could not help but sing along. Indeed, people whistled and sang along with it all the way to work that morning. When they got to work, they started dialing up the radio station and requesting Wheeler's song. The radio station happily obliged and played it frequently, quite frequently! A few days later, the *Columbia Daily Tribune* printed the words to the song in the newspaper. Friends started singing it to each other when they met on the street. "Doo doo doo doo doo doo doo" became synonymous with the town of Columbia, a ditty that stuck in each mind that heard it.

Soon, as they snapped their fingers or laughed along to the chorus, Columbians began thinking about what the song was saying. Some of them began dropping by the city council meetings, began pondering the pipeline of sewage that was going to be built, and began listening to what "those guys" Elley and Ottinger were saying. Barnett began traveling the country, researching wetlands projects and reporting on them in the newspaper. People actually felt compelled to read her articles. Then they began to feel compelled to stand up and speak out at city council meetings.

Before long city council meetings became packed with citizens engaged in heated debates lasting late into the night. Citizens became so vocal that they formed a citizens' coalition: Coalition Resolved Against the Pipeline or CRAP. CRAP grew until, with a large population base, it threatened to block the city's application for federal funding. It was a most effective move for I am sure that we are all very familiar with just how powerful CRAP can be when it decides to block something up.

It happened to be an election year. The result: a major shake up in the city council. The one member, Mary Anne McCollum, who had cast the lone dissenting vote in that now historic six-to-one night, was voted into the mayor's position.

With a new mayor and city council, folks were able to completely turn around the opinion of every state and federal agency involved: the EPA, the State Department of Conservation, the Department of Natural Resources. Agencies that had previously pooh-poohed (pardon the expression) the idea of a wetlands sewage treatment plan came around to thinking that it was not only a good idea, but that they also would provide the land and much of the funding for it.

"It was remarkable," said Forrest Rose of the *Columbia Daily Tribune*. "It just goes to show that not only can you fight city hall, but sometimes you can bring it around to your way of thinking." Black and Veatch faded into the sunset, and even the city manager came around to agreeing to the plan.

One stumbling block still existed. The city of Columbia had come up with nine million dollars, the city's part of the total financial pie and a sizable chunk of change for a town the size of Columbia. To convince people to reach into their pockets, Elley and Ottinger once again renewed their passion and professorial persuasion as Tracy Barnett launched back into her newspaper reports. Wheeler's song, though, kept Columbians singing "Doo doo doo doo doo doo doo" all the way to the polls.

When the vote came up, 95 percent of those who voted said yes to taxing themselves nine million dollars to create a wetlands sewage treatment system, an unprecedented percentage. It had been a little less than a year since Elley had first stood up. In a little less than a year, the entire situation had been turned around.

If you travel to Boone County today, you will find 120 acres of the prettiest wetlands you will ever see. Burns and McDonald, the firm who designed it, decided that 100 percent cattails would work best given the nature of Boone County's soil. So, that is what you will see when you visit. Each day, twelve million gallons of Columbia's partially treated sewage is piped into those wetlands. Then, Mother Nature goes to work, chomping away on the toxic chemicals and human waste. From the wetlands, 12 million gallons of water per day flow into the 1,300-acre Eagle Bluff Conservation District right next door, a conservation area built to mimic historic hydrological patterns of the Missouri River and which attracts migratory birds from all over the world. Without the Columbia wetlands sewage treatment system, Eagle Bluff could not exist.

Wetlands are being destroyed all over the country. Columbia is creating them. While you are visiting, you can hike the trails and spot some beautiful birds. Every once in a while, more land is added to the wetlands project. It is considered so innovative that civil engineers, like the birds, come from all over the world to take a look at it.

In Columbia though, everyone knows that it would not exist if an old hippie had not stood up; if he and a professor had not dedicated their time, passion, and persuasiveness; if a young newspaper reporter had not just kept researching and writing; and if a songwriter had not gotten irritated, penned a song, and galvanized a community. As Wheeler later said, "There's something about a song that brings a thing into real sharp focus—more than any stack of statistics or pile of pamphlets can do." He was right.

If you irritate a songwriter, you get one kind of a song. If you please a songwriter, you get something like this from Wheeler:

Talkin' Columbia City Wetland's Project
Or if you will, "Doo Doo Doo Doo Doo II"

Well, it's been a little over a year
Since I sang 'bout that wetlands imaginer.
Thanks, Doug, Hank, and Tracy for your efforts and your dreams.
This battle is part of a larger war
Fought here and there and near and far
To clean up our land, restore our rivers and our streams.

So when I order up now to quench my thirst
It's local water I ask for first,
Straight from the faucet, no bottled water please.
And I drain my glass with civic pride,
And a toast to those who have always tried
To do a little bit more than what it takes to just get by.

So the next time you flush your stool
Be thinking about us Boone County fools
With a wetlands downstream from our latrine.
We're the gem of the ocean with a capital C
With a Wetlands Project with a capital P
We boldly go where no city had gone before . . . if you know what I mean.

Now Columbia's got a newer sort of notion
What to do 'bout our dooo doo doo doo.
Yup, Columbia's got a newer sort of notion
What to do 'bout our dooo doo doo doo.

'Cause as Doug Elley says, "We all live downstream."
Yup, we . . . do!

This story is dedicated to the memory of Jerome Wheeler, 1946–2005. Wheeler and Doug Elley had been friends since the early 1960s when they were classmates at Versailles, Missouri, high school. On the day Wheeler passed on, Elley was at his bedside, holding his hand.

Beth Horner

Beth Horner has performed "The Pipeline Blues" for Live from National Geographic, the National Storytelling Festival, and NASA's Jet Propulsion Lab team. Her story has inspired remarkable citizen and environmental action elsewhere and has become a part of college coursework on political and environmental issues. Horner's performance repertoire is distinguished for its breadth: a soldier's courage in "The Silver Spurs," her mother's tenacity in "Winifred's Journey," and the hysterically funny stereotype-smashing in "Encounter with a Romance Novel." Horner is also in demand as a story consultant and teacher of narrative, structure, and the many aspects of crafting and telling good stories. For more information visit www.BethHorner.com or contact her at BethHorner@earthlink.net.

SOME CALLED HIM DOC

Lou Ann Homan

I called him Tevya. From the top of Windy Hill Farm, I watched him farm in the evenings, keeping company with the crickets and the rising of the stars. The sound of his tractor in the fields was a good-night lullaby as I latched the old screen door.

I never saw Doc wear anything but striped blue and white coveralls and muddy farm boots, but I was told he never missed a Sunday in church. His full beard covered everything but his laugh, a belly laugh, hearty and engaging. As far as I know, he never chewed or caroused, but he tinkered. He tinkered in his large red barn down the lane from Windy Hill Farm. I passed his barn every day coming home from school or late night stargazing while strolling down the lane.

In the winter the barns hibernated as the snow drifts gathered across the doors and provided insulation and warmth to the memories that lie inside. It was so quiet in the winter walking by the barns, hushed like a sleeping giant.

As the calendar slid into spring, the snow began to melt and trickle down onto the muddy road. Doc's tracks were now visible as he began to make his daily visit to the farm. As I passed on my daily journey, the doors were shut, but his old pickup was parked by the barn door as he worked through the cold spring preparing for the planting season.

Finally the day arrived—the road was dried out, the tulips bloomed, and Doc's form was visible with the barn doors wide open. Inside that barn a full museum unfolded before your eyes—tractors, steam engines, old plows, calliopes. They were lined up side by side, like babies in a nursery, wrapped in a fresh coat of paint and washed shiny and clean. They sat idly, remembering long ago. They all had stories to tell, and Doc knew all of them. As he told each story, he would touch each machine with reverence. He respected the work each had done in its time and he had restored them into good running order.

Within a summer's time each appeared to make its day in the sun. Some were so small that when he rode them, he looked like a five-year-old taking his tricycle out of the garage on the first day of spring. Doc didn't ride them anywhere really, just up and down the lane—smiling, waving, remembering.

Doc could be found at every summer parade in our small town. He was never too busy, nor was it ever too hot for him. In the early morning mist of the Fourth of July, he opened the barn door and hauled out memory after memory onto the parade route. It was easy to see that he was the favorite of the crowd—they stood and cheered as he went by. When the parade was over, we went home to Windy

Hill to eat fried chicken and to churn ice cream with fresh strawberries from the garden. There were rainbow waves of heat in the still hot air as we set up croquet or took a dip in the pond. From Windy Hill we could see Doc return home from the several parades he attended that day and put each farm piece away quietly.

It was on those hot summer days that the legend appeared—his steam engine. Once or twice a summer he would take it out of the nursery and shovel in the finest coal. It was much like the return of the prodigal son. When the engine was roaring hot, Doc would pull the whistle and ride it up and down the lane. One summer afternoon he took my three sons for a ride. He picked them up at the end of the lane. I was invited too, so I jumped right on. How often does one get the chance to ride on a steam engine? He pulled the whistle for us and laughed. We traveled through dust—through time—on that afternoon. I could imagine it was long ago and even heard the sound of long-gone thrashers. I turned around once to look to see if they were really there or just in my imagination. When the ride was over Doc beamed at his steam engine as a parent beams at a child just learning to walk.

Sometimes on summer nights, as the dusk settled, I worked in my garden, weeding carrots or tying up pole beans. Between the sounds of day ending and the darkness deepening I heard the sounds of his tractors, the pop and sputter echoing over the fields of Windy Hill. It joined in with the last bird's song. I straightened from my work to listen.

After I went into the farmhouse and washed off the day's dirt, I could still hear the laboring of his tractors going up into the fields for Doc was a night farmer. Late at night I would wrap in a blanket on the porch and watch his headlights going up and down over the hills, year after year, crop after crop. I would drink a cup of tea and listen to the creaking of the swing as I planned for a new day. I would go to sleep at night with the windows open, listening for the lullaby of his tractor.

Tevya sat on his rooftop and sang, "If I were a rich man." Doc didn't sing; his tractors did it for him. And if friends were one's riches, then Doc was the richest man I ever met.

In the late autumn when the harvest was finished, Doc would shut off the lights, quietly close the nursery door, smile, get in his pickup, and drive home.

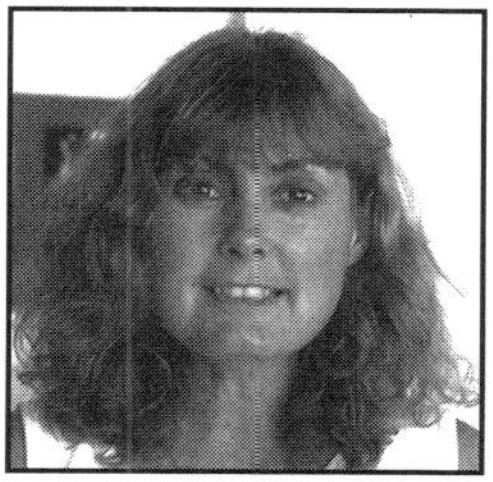
Lou Ann Homan

Lou Ann Homan can be found nestled in the hills of northern Indiana, gardening at her home at White Picket Gardens or writing late into the night under the light of her frayed scarlet lamp. She is a storyteller, a teacher, a writer, an actress, and a collector of front-porch stories, whose lyrical voice voids time and space and sends the listener's imagination dancing back to childhood. Homan takes her tales into the back roads of Indiana performing at festivals, schools, libraries, and yes, on many a front porch. For more information visit www.louannhoman.com or contact her at locketoftime@aol.com.

THE LAST FIVE MINUTES
Nancy Donoval

I grew up in a brick bungalow in the Rogers Park neighborhood on the far north side of Chicago. Many of my stories are memories of growing up in that house. Many of those memories are of the rituals that made us our own particular family such as looking ourselves up in the phone book when each new one arrived, or reading out loud on Sunday mornings—usually a book by Edgar Rice Burroughs—each of us taking a turn, chapter by chapter. Most of these family rituals revolved around my dad.

My father gave me many gifts. He gave me my sense of humor, a sense of play, and a love of words.

My father died the summer I was fifteen years old. The summer I was thirty, I was part of a performance workshop. The day we were assigned to tell family stories was the fifteenth anniversary of my father's death. On that day, he would have been with me for the first half of my life and gone for the second. A story about him seemed like a good way to put those two halves of my life together.

The times I miss my father the most are when I make new friends. I always want to introduce them to my dad because I know they would enjoy him so. A story about him is a good way of doing that as well.

****

On the afternoon of the day my father died, we went as a family to pick out his coffin. We walked down the steep, narrow stairs and into the basement showroom, but it was too hard; we couldn't do it. So instead, we decided to split up and each pick out the coffin in which we would like to be buried. I don't remember which coffin I picked, but my brother Jim picked out the best coffin. He called us all over and lined us up in front of it. It was a sleek, stylish, metallic steel-blue model that looked suspiciously like the used Toyota that he'd just bought as his first car—only no wheels and they weren't going to let him test drive it. But he made us promise that we would remember that this was the coffin that he wanted. And now, more than thirty years later as I write this, I still remember the exact shade of blue.

Jim was the one who had called us that morning, Saturday morning, from the hospital. My father had gone into a coma on Tuesday and they told us he wouldn't last the night, so we all stayed. After that first night, my family decided that since I was the baby I needed to be protected and I shouldn't stay all night again. My sister Lizzie and my brothers took turns staying but my mom was there twenty-four hours, morning, noon, night until Friday when the nurses insisted she go home to get a good night's sleep. Lizzie and Jim, being the oldest, stayed.

Jim called us the next morning at 7:00 and woke us up and said, "Why don't you eat breakfast and come on down."

He called back at 7:15 and said, "Don't eat breakfast. Come on down."

So we piled into our blue Chevy station wagon and headed to the hospital. I don't remember who was driving, my mother or my brother Joe. They'd both gotten their drivers' licenses within the last few months Joe at eighteen and Mom at forty-eight and it was a toss-up as to which of them we felt safest with behind the wheel. They got into the front seat to team drive and I curled up in the backseat and went back to sleep. I went to sleep on my dad's green corduroy, foam-stuffed TV pillow. He had a really bad back and he would use this pillow under his knees when he was watching TV in bed.

****

I grew up in a TV family. We had TVs in almost every room in the house. But the best TV was the one in my parents' bedroom—right at the foot of their bed. What made it so great was that this was one of the very first TVs that had a remote control.

The remote was a little square tin box that had one big button coming up out of it at an angle. If you were a little kid like I was when we first got it, you'd need both thumbs to push the button down. And when you did it would make this really loud clicking sound. That's what we called it. The clicker. Push the button on the clicker once and it would turn the TV on. Click it again and the TV would turn off. Click on. Click off. If you wanted to change the volume or watch one of the other six channels, you had to crawl to the end of the bed and turn the dial. But that didn't matter. You could turn the TV on and off from the doorway of the room. It was amazing!

And my dad could work miracles with the TV. One of them went like this. Because of his bad back, he had a back brace he had to wear all the time. It was a dirty manila envelope color, with thick metal stays, laces in the back to pull it tight, and big metal snaps down the front.

Dad would have the back brace on and he'd go into the living room. Joe and I would go upstairs to our parents' bedroom, which was right over the living room.

We'd stomp on the floor so that Dad would know we were ready. When he got the signal, my father would grip the top edges of the back brace and he would rip it open like Clark Kent turning into Superman. If he opened at just the right speed, at just the right angle, so all those metal snaps popped just the right way . . . it would turn the TV on upstairs. Right through the floor. It was a miracle!

Joey and I would pound on the floor so that he knew it had worked and he would snap back up. We'd click off the TV and he'd do it again. And again. And again. We could spend a very pleasant Saturday afternoon that way. Working miracles.

Dad could work other miracles with the TV. He could work the miracle of getting our mother to let us stay up late on a school night to watch TV with him.

It was always on a Monday. Joe and I would come right home from school; we'd do all our homework before supper. After dinner, we had to go straight to bed, sleep fast, and sleep hard. Then, at 10:25, Dad would wake us up to watch the 10:30 movie with him. My mother would say, "Richard, they are children, they need eight hours sleep." And he would say, "They're getting eight hours, they're just getting it in two batches." And that was that.

Why Mondays? Was that the night PBS showed films like *The Grapes of Wrath* or *War and Peace?* Oh, no. When I was a kid growing up in Chicago, Monday nights on Channel 9 WGN was *Creature Features* night. Our dad was waking us up so that we could keep him company watching *Frankenstein* or *The Wolfman* or *Frankenstein Meets the Wolfman* or the one that really scared me, *The Brain That Wouldn't Die.*

There was one rule. If Dad had worked this hard to get us to be able to stay up late, we had to stay awake. We had to stay awake. If you fell asleep in the middle of the movie, he wouldn't tell you what happened—and he wouldn't let anyone else tell you either. Even if all you did was doze off right at the end of the movie and miss the last five minutes, then jerk awake as the credits were rolling, it didn't matter. You could beg, you could plead, but all my father would do was look you straight in the eye—a man who had never lied in his life, the soul of honesty—and say, "Everybody died and went to heaven."

That was that. You wouldn't get anything else out of him. It was his favorite joke, but it sure taught me. I got really good at staying awake. I can stay awake through pretty much anything. My brother Joey did not develop this skill, and it is possible he still thinks that all the movies made during the 1930s, 1940s, and 1950s, especially the Hammer and Universal horror films, end with everybody dying and going to heaven.

****

We didn't watch a lot of TV in the hospital for a couple of reasons. When my dad went in that last time, the other bed in his room was already occupied. The man in it was in even worse shape than my dad. I never really knew what had made him sick, but he'd been in a coma for a long time and before that his eyesight had failed and he'd gone completely blind. The curtain between the two beds was always pulled. His family would be there but it was always really quiet on the other side of the curtain. My mom would say, "Be respectful," and she didn't want us to play the TV too loudly or too often in case it bothered them.

The other reason that we didn't watch much TV was because at the same time that we had to say good-bye to our father, he was struggling to say good-bye to himself. He had always been the smartest, funniest, quickest person I'd ever known and all of that was slipping away. He was losing pieces of himself every day and every day he would try to grab on to them and pull them back. Mostly it was by asking questions.

One afternoon when I was alone in the room with him he asked me, "What's the Law of Supply and Demand?"

I had no idea what he was talking about. I had just finished my freshman year at St. Scholastica Academy for Young Ladies and economic principles had not been part of the curriculum. But my father had been a business major in college and then had worked as an operations secretary for a breading company, the company that invented ice-cream cake roll, for twenty-five years. Supply and demand had been fundamental to his work life and he knew he should know what it was but he couldn't remember. And I couldn't tell him.

It wasn't until years later that I realized that that afternoon in my father's hospital room was my first economics lesson. My father demanded something of me that I did not have in supply. And yet, I had an endless supply of the last five minutes of movies from the 1930s, 1940s, and 1950s, which I'd stayed awake for. Only that was no longer in demand.

****

I slept on my father's green corduroy, foam-stuffed TV pillow on the way to the hospital and I could sleep because I knew something that nobody else in my family knew. I knew my father was not going to die. I knew because I had been praying.

I was raised intensely Catholic and I was the kind of kid who believed everything.

When I was eight, I was convinced the whole world was divided into "Catholic" and "Public." Every kid I knew either went to St. Margaret Mary (the Catholic school) or Armstrong (the public school) so I thought those were the two major religions. Then, we started learning how at the end of the world, on Judgment Day, the Publics were in big trouble. But it was okay because it was part of our job as Catholics to "Spread the Word." It was around this time that I started to realize that my friends from the local YMCA, Jeannie Niederman and Barbara Siegel, were Publics and they were in danger.

That's when I got invited to have dinner at Barbara's house for the first time. Barbara was my water ballet partner and I loved her. We were in sync. So I went over to her house for dinner and I spent the whole meal trying to convert Barbara's entire family from Judaism to Catholicism. At the end of the evening, when my dad came to pick me up, Mrs. Siegel walked me to the door, put her arm around me and told me that I was welcome at their house anytime I wanted to come. That was the end of my missionary career. But I still believed everything.

****

When I was fifteen, what I believed in was, "Ask and you shall receive." I believed that if I had enough time to say enough prayers and that if I believed, really believed, I would get a miracle and my father wouldn't die. So I could sleep on his green corduroy, foam-stuffed TV pillow on the way to the hospital.

When we got there, we walked into his room and my eyes went right to my father's face. If you've ever been around someone who's been really sick, you know that they stop looking like themselves. My dad hadn't looked like himself for a long time. Plus, he'd worn an oxygen mask for the last week and we hadn't been able to really see his face that well. But now the mask was gone and there was my dad. He wore the face that I had grown up loving and hadn't seen in so long. And my first thought was, "Yes! Yes! I got a miracle!"

Then I looked around the room, at my mom, at Lizzie, Jim, and Joe. I looked back at my dad's face and I realized what had happened. I had finally fallen asleep and missed the last five minutes. I had missed the moment when my father's favorite joke became absolute truth. Everybody dies and everybody goes to heaven.

I started to cry. The nurses hustled me out and they decided that what I needed to comfort me was a glass of milk. I think they all got their nurse's training in Wisconsin. It was difficult in those days to get anything out of the hospital kitchen when it wasn't feeding time, but those nurses were valiant. They got me that glass of milk and I drank it, and I think that maybe they felt a little better.

Then I went back into my father's room. Our side of the room was really, really quiet.

But on the other side of the curtain there was all sorts of commotion going on. I found out later that morning that my father's roommate had woken up. He'd opened his eyes and he could see.

That afternoon, my family went to pick out the coffins we wanted to be buried in. But that other family—they spent the afternoon celebrating the miracle they had received.

****

My father gave me many gifts. He gave me my sense of humor, a sense of play, and a love of words. In giving me these gifts, he gave me storytelling, which is the way I have to give him to you.

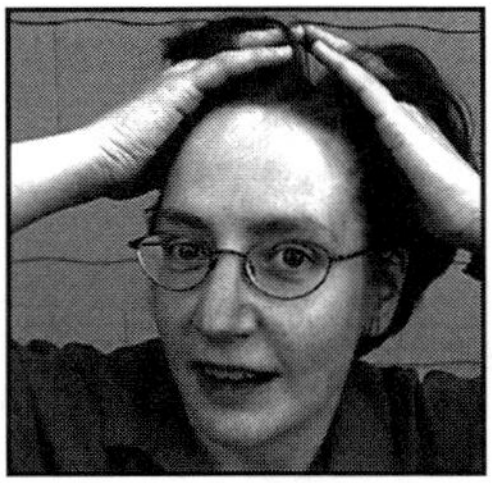

Nancy Donoval

Nancy Donoval was born and raised in Chicago where many of her stories take place. She was featured at the 2004 National Storytelling Festival in Jonesborough, Tennessee. Other venues include the Timpanogos Storytelling Festival, New York Storytelling Center, Washington Storytellers Theater, and the Illinois, Hoosier, and Nebraska Storytelling Festivals. With a master of fine arts degree in directing from Northwestern University, Donoval is a respected story coach and corporate consultant with clients such as Leo Burnett, Draft, and Character LLC. She teaches storytelling at Metropolitan State University in her current home of Minneapolis and leads workshops on crafting autobiographical stories around the country for performers and other public speakers. For more information visit www.storynet.org/tellers/NancyDonoval.htm or contact her at nancystories@yahoo.com.

THE RAINMAKER
Michael Cotter

When you live off the land as I do, and we've had the same address for 120 years, I think the word that is most terrifying is the word "drought"—that time when the rains just will not come.

The story is told of a village in ancient China that was experiencing a drought. In that time they did not have transportation options to move grain or people, and so when a village experienced drought, they worried. And if the drought was severe, they died.

This village prayed first to their ancestors, as was their custom, but no rain fell. Then they paraded their sacred images through the drought-stricken fields. Still no rain came. Finally in desperation, they sent far afield for a rainmaker, and when he came trudging up the path of the village in the evening, they were very disappointed.

They expected someone powerful and young. Instead, a little man with a thin, white beard and stooped shoulders came trudging toward them. They asked him what he needed to work his wonders. He said simply, "A place to live." They gave him a hut at the edge of the village, and there he went about doing the things necessary for one to live. On the third day the rain came.

I believe in all of our lives, there come periods of drought, but I believe rainmakers are sent, and I'll tell you why I feel that way.

When I was in my early thirties, my father was very old and was getting ready to die.

He had held the power of the purse and control of our farm with a heavy hand; and now in his late eighties, he just needed to let go. For the first time, I was going to have a chance to make that farm powerful, the way I knew it should be.

I had gotten larger machinery, was running larger acreage, and had two full-time employees.

One summer afternoon, a man came and asked me for a job. I probably wouldn't have hired him except that I'd heard his story. His name was Ed, and he had white hair and very thick glasses. He was sixty-five, his shoulders were stooped, and I saw him then as an old man—now I would call him middle-aged.

The story that I knew was that a few years earlier, when he was a successful dairy farmer on a small farm, Ed had discovered that he had cancer. He called his grown children together, his wife having died several years earlier, to see if anyone wanted to take over the little farm and his wonderful herd of dairy cows. None of the three children were interested, so the farm and all of its equipment was sold, and Ed went to the Veterans Hospital in Minneapolis. After a series of operations, Ed got well, and he always seemed to treat life as a gift.

This is what he said to me that day. "If I would be any help to you, I would sure appreciate the job."

Fifteen years later, Ed was eighty. He had been sick a lot that year. It was late fall, and he was trying to stay with me through the harvest. Ed always gave a full measure of himself, so he was trying to finish the plowing, even though the snow was coming down.

By now we had the four-wheel-drive tractors, with the eight big tires, and the cabs that sat high off the ground. Ed was coming in through the snow, his face white behind the windshield. The snow was melting on the hood of that tractor and the water was running off of it. He was finished plowing, he was trying to park that tractor, and he seemed to need help.

I went over by the tractor as he shut it off, because everything was slippery on that deck; and as Ed started climbing down, he slipped, and I was there to catch him.

In that vulnerable moment, this is what he said to me. "You need a better man than me now. I sure have appreciated the job."

In those fifteen years Ed taught me so much. When he first came, I didn't ask Ed for advice, and he didn't volunteer any. I'd spent my whole life with old men, and I knew that when they started giving advice, they sometimes forgot to stop.

Then I began to notice something. Ed always gave a full measure. When he prepared some land, whether it was wet or dry, he always seemed to leave that soil as good as it could be. He seemed to have a way with the land. When we would plant in the spring—and by now we were planting about nine hundred acres—I would move Ed's tractor in close to mine, so I always planted in land that was prepared as good as it could be.

With Ed there, I began to see the sun and to notice the day, and for fifteen years that was how I planted, because Ed was always there and he always gave a full measure. I began to ask his advice and to depend on it.

His advice was always brief, and he always ended it the same way. "You're the one who has to decide," he would say. "You're the boss."

My mother lived in a house on that farm, and my new house was built behind it in the woods. By this time my dad had been gone for many years, and she was getting old. She had a full view of the farmyard, and I stopped to see her each morning.

If she was not feeling well, or if the weather was bad, she would look out and see something in that farmyard she didn't like and tell me that I was a poor manager. This would upset me and I would have to talk to Ed. He would give me his little smile and his words of wisdom. He'd say, "Mothers are supposed to say that. That's their job in life. It keeps you humble. That's what they're supposed to do."

And then in some way, he would tell me that I was a good manager, and then he would do everything he could to make me look like one.

When there were difficult jobs or difficult people to work with, I would say, "Ed, can you handle this?" and he'd smile that little smile and say, "You know, I guess I've been lucky. That sort of thing (or that sort of person) never did bodder me much." He always said "bodder."

Ed had been gassed in the First World War, so breathing was a little difficult for him. When he came home from the war, he got a job as a welder, but he didn't have good glasses to protect his eyes, and they were burned very badly. So he had these very thick glasses to make up for the damage his eyes had received. His wife had died of leukemia after a long and expensive illness. Ed himself had had cancer a few years later. But when he spoke, he said, "I've really been lucky. Life has been good." And he meant it.

Ed did have a gift that few have. When I had a success, he enjoyed it like it was his own. And a person like that has much joy in life.

Ed died within a year after he left me, and our farm never recovered from his leaving.

On the day of his funeral, there was another man being buried also—someone more important in the community than Ed. The pastor was in a hurry, and I could see what was going to happen. He was going to say that Ed was a good man, and that was about it, because the pastor didn't know him at all.

I couldn't let that happen, so I asked the family for permission to speak a few words.

I told the story of the rainmaker. I said, "Ed was an extraordinary man, and for me, he had been a rainmaker. He always gave a full measure."

I looked out on the crowd, many of Ed's old neighbors when he farmed. Their eyes and their faces held affirmation. "Yes, that was the Ed we knew." I said how Ed had a way with growing things, and that he gave me courage when I needed it.

I looked down upon Ed's family, and for the most part, they too were affirming me with their eyes. But his oldest son looked at me with dark eyes blazing with anger. I remembered what Ed said. "I could get along with about any man, but I never seemed to make it with my boy."

I thought of how Ed had been a rainmaker for me, but he probably hadn't yet learned that skill when his boy needed him, so the son hadn't gotten the gift that I had. As I left the funeral that day, those angry eyes haunted me, and then I remembered the story of the rainmaker.

At times, we have to send far afield for our rainmaker, and when he comes, we sometimes don't recognize him.

I believe that, in all of our lives, there come periods of drought, but I believe rainmakers are sent. So watch for your rainmaker. Remember, they make barely a ripple when they come.

Michael Cotter

Michael Cotter was born on a farm in the Great Depression and grew up during the Second World War. He is the youngest of a family of eight, and after taking over management of the farm, he helped it to triple in size and evolve from draft horses to modern powered equipment. He was introduced to storytelling at age fifty, and it became a powerful force in his life. He has appeared on college campuses, at high school graduations, hospitals, churches, the Smithsonian Institution, theaters, festivals, including the National Storytelling Festival, agricultural seminars, conventions, and on radio, television, and video productions. Contact him at 50201 205th St., Austin MN 55912 or 507-437-3306.